REMARKABLE 2

USER/MANUAL GUIDE

A Step-by-Step Guide to Using Your reMarkable 2

NORMAN C. SIMMONS

Disclaimer

The information contained in this book is intended for general information purposes only and does not constitute professional advice. The author makes no representations or warranties, express or implied, as to the accuracy, reliability, or completeness of the information contained herein. The author shall not be liable for any loss or damage of any kind arising from the use of or reliance on any of the information presented in this book.

TABLE OF CONTENTS

INTRODUCTION...2

CHAPTER 1..5

Getting Started...5

- Charging and powering on...5
- Setting up your reMarkable 2...8
- Connecting to Wi-Fi..11
- Creating a reMarkable account..14
- Navigating the interface..17
- Basic gestures and controls..20
- Understanding the toolbar and menus...22

CHAPTER 2..27

The Basics of Note-Taking...27

- Creating your first notebook...27
- Choosing templates and covers..30
- Using the different writing tools (pens, markers, pencils)...................................34
- Adjusting stroke thickness and color...37
- Erasing and undoing mistakes...39
- Inserting and manipulating shapes..41
- Working with layers..44

CHAPTER 3..47

Advanced Note-Taking Techniques...47

- Converting handwriting to text..47
- Searching your notes...50
- Organizing notebooks with folders and tags..54

Organizing Notebooks with Folders and Tags on the reMarkable 2............................57

- Creating tables and lists...60
- Annotating PDFs and ebooks...62

CHAPTER 4..65

Working with Documents...65

- Importing PDFs and ebooks..66
- Annotating and marking up documents..70
- Exporting documents as PDF, PNG, or SVG..73
- Using the reMarkable desktop app..76
- Integrating with cloud services (Google Drive, Dropbox, etc.)...............................79

CHAPTER 5..82

Beyond Note-Taking...82

- Using the reMarkable 2 as a sketchbook..83

● Creating digital planners and journals...86

● Managing to-do lists and tasks...89

● Reading and annotating sheet music...91

● Using the reMarkable 2 for presentations..95

CHAPTER 6..**99**

Customization and Settings..**99**

● Personalizing your device settings...99

● Adjusting display and power settings...102

● Managing storage and backups..107

● Updating the reMarkable 2 software..110

● Troubleshooting common issues...112

CHAPTER 7..**117**

Tips and Tricks...**117**

● Maximizing battery life..117

● Optimizing your workflow...120

● Exploring hidden features..122

● Using third-party accessories...125

● Joining the reMarkable community..127

CONCLUSION..**130**

INTRODUCTION

Welcome to the world of the reMarkable 2, a digital device designed to bridge the gap between traditional paper and modern technology. This guide will take you through the essentials of the reMarkable 2, explaining its purpose, key features, and what you can expect when you first unbox it.

What is the reMarkable 2 and Who is it For?

The reMarkable 2 isn't just another tablet. It's a digital notebook designed for focused work, free from the distractions of notifications, apps, and the constant pull of the internet. It offers a unique writing experience that closely mimics the feel of pen on paper, making it an ideal tool for:

- **Students:** Taking notes in lectures, annotating PDFs of research papers, and organizing study materials.
- **Professionals:** Brainstorming ideas, sketching diagrams, reviewing documents, and managing projects.
- **Writers:** Drafting manuscripts, outlining stories, and editing their work in a distraction-free environment.
- **Creatives:** Sketching, drawing, and expressing their artistic vision.
- **Anyone seeking focused work:** Those who value deep work and want to minimize digital distractions.

The reMarkable 2 is for those who appreciate the tactile feel of writing and drawing but desire the convenience and organizational benefits of digital technology. It's for those who want to reclaim focus in a world of constant digital noise.

Key Features and Benefits:

The reMarkable 2 offers a unique combination of features that set it apart:

- **Paper-Like Writing Experience:** The CANVAS display technology and textured surface provide a tactile feel that closely resembles writing on paper. The low latency ensures minimal lag between pen stroke and digital ink, creating a fluid and responsive writing experience.
- **Distraction-Free Environment:** With no email, social media, or web browser, the reMarkable 2 encourages focused work and deep concentration.
- **Organization and Accessibility:** Digital notes are easily searchable, organized into notebooks and folders, and accessible across devices through the reMarkable cloud.

- **Versatile Functionality:** Beyond note-taking, the reMarkable 2 supports PDF annotation, ebook reading, and sketching, making it a versatile tool for various tasks.
- **Long Battery Life:** The reMarkable 2 boasts impressive battery life, allowing for days of use on a single charge.
- **Sleek and Minimalist Design:** The thin and lightweight design makes it highly portable and comfortable to hold.

Unboxing and First Impressions:

Opening the reMarkable 2 box is a premium experience. The packaging is minimalist and elegant, reflecting the device's design philosophy. Inside, you'll find:

- **The reMarkable 2 tablet:** The device itself, with its sleek, dark grey finish and minimalist design.
- **The Marker (or Marker Plus if purchased):** The stylus that allows you to write and draw on the device. The Marker Plus includes an eraser on the back.
- **USB-C Cable:** For charging and connecting to your computer.
- **Quick Start Guide:** A brief guide to get you started.

Upon holding the reMarkable 2 for the first time, you'll immediately notice its slim profile and lightweight feel. The textured surface of the display is immediately apparent, hinting at the paper-like writing experience.

Technical Specifications:

- **Display:** 10.3-inch monochrome digital paper display (CANVAS display technology)
- **Resolution:** 1872 x 1404 (226 DPI)
- **Processor:** 1.2 GHz dual-core ARM processor
- **Storage:** 8 GB internal storage
- **RAM:** 1 GB
- **Connectivity:** Wi-Fi (2.4 GHz and 5 GHz)
- **Battery:** Rechargeable lithium-ion battery (up to two weeks of use)
- **Dimensions:** 188 x 246 x 4.7 mm (7.4 x 9.7 x 0.19 inches)
- **Weight:** Approximately 403.5 g (0.89 lbs)

Initial Setup (What to Press):

1. **Powering On:** Press and hold the power button located on the top edge of the device (it's a small, circular button). The reMarkable logo will appear, indicating that the device is starting up.

2. **Language Selection:** Once the device powers on, you will be greeted with a language selection screen. Use the Marker to tap on your preferred language.

3. **Wi-Fi Connection:** The reMarkable 2 will then prompt you to connect to a Wi-Fi network. Tap on your network name from the list and enter your password using the on-screen keyboard. Tap the checkmark icon to confirm.

4. **reMarkable Account:** You'll be asked to create or sign in to a reMarkable account. This is essential for syncing your notes and accessing other features. If you don't have an account, tap "Create account" and follow the on-screen instructions. If you already have an account, tap "Sign in" and enter your credentials.

5. **Tutorial:** The reMarkable 2 will then guide you through a brief interactive tutorial demonstrating basic gestures and features. Pay attention to this tutorial as it will introduce you to the core functionalities of the device. This tutorial will guide you through using the marker on the screen, selecting tools from the toolbar, and navigating the interface.

Once you've completed these steps, you'll be on the main screen, ready to start using your reMarkable 2. This initial setup process is straightforward and intuitive, designed to get you up and running quickly.

CHAPTER 1

<u>Getting Started</u>

This chapter covers the essential first steps, from powering on your device for the first time to understanding the user interface. We'll guide you through the initial setup process, including charging, connecting to Wi-Fi, and creating your reMarkable account. We'll then explore the device's navigation, introducing you to basic gestures and controls that will become second nature as you use your reMarkable 2.

Charging and powering on

The reMarkable 2 is equipped with a rechargeable lithium-ion battery designed to provide extended usage. The actual battery life will vary depending on usage patterns, such as frequency of writing, Wi-Fi usage, and screen brightness. However, under typical use, you can expect several days of use on a single charge.

What You'll Need:

- **reMarkable 2 Device:** Your new reMarkable 2 tablet.
- **USB-C Cable:** The cable included in the reMarkable 2 box. This cable is specifically designed for charging and data transfer.
- **USB Power Adapter (Optional):** While you can charge your reMarkable 2 by connecting it to a computer's USB port, using a wall adapter (like the one you use for your phone) will generally provide faster charging. Ensure the adapter is a reputable brand and complies with standard safety regulations. A 5V/2A (10W) adapter is recommended for optimal charging speed.

Charging Your reMarkable 2:

1. **Locate the USB-C Port:** The USB-C port is located on the bottom edge of the reMarkable 2, in the center.

2. **Connect the Cable:** Insert the USB-C end of the cable into the port on your reMarkable 2.

3. **Connect to a Power Source:**

   - **Using a Wall Adapter:** Connect the other end of the USB-C cable to your USB power adapter. Plug the adapter into a wall outlet.

- Using a Computer: Connect the other end of the USB-C cable to a USB port on your computer. Ensure your computer is powered on.

4. **Charging Indication:** Once connected to a power source, the reMarkable 2's screen will display a charging indicator. This indicator typically shows a battery icon with a lightning bolt symbol or a percentage indicating the current charge level.

5. **Charging Time:** The time it takes to fully charge your reMarkable 2 will depend on the power source you are using. Charging via a wall adapter will generally be faster than charging via a computer's USB port. A full charge can take approximately 2-3 hours with a suitable wall adapter.

6. **Charging Status:**

   - **Charging:** The battery icon will animate or the percentage will increase, indicating that the device is actively charging.
   - **Fully Charged:** Once the battery is fully charged, the charging indicator will typically show a full battery icon or 100%. Some devices might display a message indicating that charging is complete.

Important Charging Considerations:

- **Using Third-Party Cables and Adapters:** While you can use third-party USB-C cables and adapters, it is strongly recommended to use the cable provided with your reMarkable 2 or a high-quality, certified cable from a reputable brand. Using low-quality or non compliant cables and adapters can potentially damage your device or result in slower charging.
- **Charging Temperature:** Avoid charging your reMarkable 2 in extreme temperatures (very hot or very cold). Optimal charging occurs at room temperature.
- **Overcharging:** Modern lithium-ion batteries, like the one in the reMarkable 2, have built-in protection against overcharging. However, it's generally good practice to unplug your device once it's fully charged.
- **First-Time Charging:** It's not necessary to fully charge your reMarkable 2 before using it for the first time, as it usually ships with some charge. However, allowing it to reach a full charge initially can help calibrate the battery meter.

Powering On Your reMarkable 2:

Once your reMarkable 2 has sufficient charge (even a small amount will do for the initial setup), you can power it on:

1. **Locate the Power Button:** The power button is a small, circular button located on the top edge of the device, typically on the left side when holding it in portrait orientation.
2. **Press and Hold:** Press and hold the power button for approximately 2-3 seconds.
3. **reMarkable Logo:** The screen will initially go black, then the reMarkable logo will appear, indicating that the device is powering on.
4. **Boot-Up Sequence:** After the logo, the device will proceed through its boot-up sequence, which may take a few moments.
5. **Initial Setup Screens:** The first time you power on your reMarkable 2, you will be guided through the initial setup process, which includes selecting your language, connecting to Wi-Fi, and creating or signing in to your reMarkable account. These steps are crucial for accessing the device's full functionality.

Powering Off Your reMarkable 2:

1. **Press and Hold:** Press and hold the power button for approximately 3 seconds.
2. **Power Off Options:** A menu will appear on the screen with options to "Turn off" or "Cancel."
3. **Select "Turn off":** Use the Marker to tap on the "Turn off" option. The device will then shut down.

Putting Your reMarkable 2 to Sleep:

To conserve battery life when not actively using your reMarkable 2, you can put it to sleep:

1. **Short Press:** Briefly press the power button once.
2. **Sleep Screen:** The screen will display a "reMarkable is sleeping" message, indicating that the device is in sleep mode.
3. **Waking Up:** To wake the device, briefly press the power button again.

By following these instructions, you can ensure that your reMarkable 2 is properly charged and powered on, allowing you to begin your digital paper journey seamlessly.

After powering on your reMarkable 2 for the first time, you will be greeted by a series of setup screens designed to personalize your device and connect it to the reMarkable services.

1. Language Selection:

- **What you'll see:** A screen displaying a list of available languages.
- **What to do:** Use your Marker to tap on your preferred language. This will set the device's interface language.
- **Why it's important:** Choosing the correct language ensures that all menus, settings, and on-screen text are displayed in a language you understand.

2. Connecting to Wi-Fi:

- **What you'll see:** A screen displaying a list of available Wi-Fi networks.
- **What to do:**
  - **Select your network:** Tap on the name of your Wi-Fi network from the list.
  - **Enter your password:** An on-screen keyboard will appear. Use your Marker to tap on the keys to enter your Wi-Fi password. The keyboard includes standard letters, numbers, and symbols.
  - **Confirm:** Once you have entered your password, tap the checkmark icon (usually located in the bottom right corner of the keyboard) to confirm.
- **Why it's important:** Connecting to Wi-Fi is essential for syncing your notes to the reMarkable cloud, downloading software updates, and accessing other online features.

Troubleshooting Wi-Fi Connection:

- **Network not listed:** If your network isn't listed, ensure that your Wi-Fi router is turned on and broadcasting its SSID (network name). You may need to move closer to the router to improve the signal strength. If your network is hidden, you may have an option on the remarkable to manually enter the SSID.
- **Incorrect password:** If you enter the wrong password, the reMarkable 2 will display an error message. Double-check your password and try again.
- **Connection issues:** If you are still having trouble connecting, try restarting your Wi-Fi router and your reMarkable 2.

3. Creating or Signing in to a reMarkable Account:

- **What you'll see:** A screen prompting you to either create a new reMarkable account or sign in to an existing one.
- **What to do:**
  - **Creating a new account:** Tap "Create account". You will be asked to provide:
    - **Email address:** Enter a valid email address that you have access to.
    - **Password:** Create a strong password that you can remember.
  - **Signing in to an existing account:** Tap "Sign in". You will be asked to provide:
    - **Email address:** Enter the email address associated with your reMarkable account.
    - **Password:** Enter your reMarkable account password.
- **Why it's important:** A reMarkable account is necessary for syncing your notes across devices, backing up your data, and accessing features like the reMarkable desktop and mobile apps.

4. Terms and Conditions:

- **What you'll see:** A screen displaying the reMarkable Terms and Conditions and Privacy Policy.
- **What to do:** Read through the terms and conditions. If you agree, tap "Accept".
- **Why it's important:** Accepting the terms and conditions is required to use the reMarkable services.

5. Interactive Tutorial:

- **What you'll see:** A short interactive tutorial demonstrating basic gestures and features of the reMarkable 2.
- **What to do:** Follow the on-screen instructions and use your Marker to interact with the device. This tutorial will cover:
  - **Basic writing and erasing:** Practicing writing and erasing with the Marker.
  - **Selecting tools from the toolbar:** Learning how to choose different pens, markers, and other tools.
  - **Navigating the interface:** Getting familiar with basic navigation gestures.
- **Why it's important:** This tutorial is a great way to get acquainted with the reMarkable 2's interface and core functionalities.

6. Welcome Screen:

- **What you'll see:** A welcome screen indicating that the setup process is complete.
- **What to do:** Tap "Get started" to proceed to the main interface.

Post-Setup Actions:

After completing the initial setup, there are a few additional steps you can take to further personalize your reMarkable 2 experience:

- **Explore the settings:** Familiarize yourself with the device's settings menu, which allows you to customize various aspects of the device, such as display settings, Wi-Fi connections, and account information.
- **Download the desktop and mobile apps:** The reMarkable desktop and mobile apps allow you to access your notes on your computer and smartphone, providing seamless syncing and access across devices. Download these apps from the reMarkable website or your device's app store.
- **Explore templates:** The reMarkable 2 comes with a variety of pre-installed templates for different purposes, such as note-taking, sketching, and planning. Explore these templates and choose the ones that best suit your needs.

Troubleshooting Setup Issues:

- **Device freezes:** If your reMarkable 2 freezes during the setup process, try performing a hard reset by holding down the power button for about 10 seconds.
- **Account creation issues:** If you have trouble creating a reMarkable account, ensure that you are using a valid email address and that your password meets the required criteria.
- **Syncing problems:** If your notes are not syncing correctly after setup, check your Wi-Fi connection and ensure that you are signed in to the correct reMarkable account on all your devices.

By following these steps, you can successfully set up your reMarkable 2 and begin enjoying its unique digital paper experience. This initial setup ensures that your device is configured correctly and connected to the reMarkable ecosystem, allowing you to take full advantage of its features.

- *Connecting to Wi-Fi*

Connecting your reMarkable 2 to Wi-Fi is a crucial step in setting up and maximizing the device's functionality. A stable Wi-Fi connection enables essential features like cloud syncing, software updates, and access to the reMarkable desktop and mobile apps. This guide provides a detailed walkthrough of connecting your reMarkable 2 to Wi-Fi, troubleshooting common issues, and understanding Wi-Fi management on the device.

Why Wi-Fi is Important for Your reMarkable 2:

- **Cloud Syncing:** Wi-Fi allows your notes, documents, and other files to be automatically synced to the reMarkable cloud. This ensures that your work is backed up and accessible from other devices via the reMarkable apps.
- **Software Updates:** reMarkable regularly releases software updates that improve performance, add new features, and fix bugs. These updates are delivered over Wi-Fi.
- **Desktop and Mobile Apps:** The reMarkable desktop and mobile apps require an internet connection to sync with your device. This connection is facilitated through Wi-Fi on your reMarkable 2.
- **Firmware Updates for Accessories:** If you use accessories like the Marker Plus, firmware updates for these may be delivered over Wi-Fi.

Connecting to Wi-Fi During Initial Setup:

As covered in the previous section on setting up your reMarkable 2, connecting to Wi-Fi is typically part of the initial setup process. Here's a recap with more detail:

1. **Wi-Fi Selection Screen:** After selecting your language during the initial setup, you'll be presented with a screen displaying available Wi-Fi networks.

2. **Scanning for Networks:** The reMarkable 2 will automatically scan for nearby Wi-Fi networks. This process may take a few seconds.

3. **Network List:** A list of detected Wi-Fi networks will appear on the screen, showing their names (SSIDs).

4. **Selecting Your Network (What to Press):**

   ○ Use your Marker to tap directly on the name (SSID) of the Wi-Fi network you wish to connect to.

5. **Entering Your Password (What to Press):**

   ○ After selecting a network, an on-screen keyboard will appear.
   ○ Use your Marker to tap on the keys to enter your Wi-Fi password. The keyboard includes uppercase and lowercase letters (accessible by tapping the shift key), numbers, and symbols.

- If you make a mistake, use the backspace key (usually located on the right side of the keyboard) to delete characters.
- Once you've entered the complete password, tap the checkmark or "Connect" button (usually located in the bottom right corner of the keyboard).

6. **Connection Attempt:** The reMarkable 2 will attempt to connect to the selected Wi-Fi network. A brief message will appear indicating the connection status.

7. **Successful Connection:** If the connection is successful, a Wi-Fi icon will appear in the top status bar of the reMarkable 2's screen, typically showing the signal strength.

Connecting to Wi-Fi After Initial Setup:

If you skipped connecting to Wi-Fi during the initial setup or need to connect to a different network later, you can do so through the settings menu:

1. **Accessing the Settings Menu (What to Press):**

   - From the main screen (where your notebooks and documents are displayed), swipe down from the top of the screen to open the quick settings menu.
   - Tap the gear icon (Settings) in the top right corner of the quick settings menu.
2. **Navigating to Wi-Fi Settings (What to Press):**

   - In the Settings menu, tap on "Wi-Fi".
3. **Connecting to a Network (What to Press):**

   - The Wi-Fi settings screen will display a list of available networks.
   - Ensure the Wi-Fi toggle is switched on (if it isn't, tap it to enable Wi-Fi).
   - Tap on the name of the network you want to connect to.
   - Enter the Wi-Fi password using the on-screen keyboard as described above, and then tap the checkmark or "Connect" button.

Managing Saved Wi-Fi Networks:

The reMarkable 2 remembers the Wi-Fi networks you've connected to. You can manage these saved networks in the Wi-Fi settings:

1. **Access the Wi-Fi Settings (as described above).**

2. **Viewing Saved Networks:** The Wi-Fi settings screen will list the saved networks.

3. **Forgetting a Network (What to Press):**

    ○ Tap on the name of the saved network you want to forget.
    ○ A screen with network details will appear.
    ○ Tap the "Forget network" option. This will remove the saved password for that network.

Troubleshooting Wi-Fi Connection Issues:

- **Incorrect Password:** Double-check that you are entering the correct Wi-Fi password. Passwords are case-sensitive.
- **Weak Signal:** If the Wi-Fi signal is weak, try moving closer to your Wi-Fi router.
- **Router Issues:** Restart your Wi-Fi router. This often resolves temporary network problems.
-
- **reMarkable 2 Restart:** Restart your reMarkable 2 by holding down the power button for about 10 seconds.
- **Network Congestion:** If many devices are using the same Wi-Fi network, it can cause congestion and connection problems. Try disconnecting some devices or using a different network if available.
- **Hidden Network:** If your network's SSID is hidden, you'll need to manually add it:
    ○ In the Wi-Fi settings, look for an option like "Add network" or "+".
    ○ You'll be prompted to enter the network name (SSID), security type (e.g., WPA2), and password.

Wi-Fi Security Considerations:

- **Use Strong Passwords:** Use a strong and unique password for your Wi-Fi network to protect your data.
- **WPA2/WPA3 Encryption:** Ensure your Wi-Fi router is using WPA2 or the more recent WPA3 encryption for enhanced security.

A reMarkable account is essential for unlocking the full potential of your reMarkable 2. It enables cloud syncing, access to the reMarkable desktop and mobile apps, and provides a secure backup of your valuable notes and documents. This comprehensive guide details the process of creating a reMarkable account, troubleshooting potential issues, and understanding the benefits it offers.

Why You Need a reMarkable Account:

- **Cloud Syncing and Backup:** Your reMarkable account is the cornerstone of the reMarkable cloud service. It automatically backs up your notes, notebooks, and other files to the cloud, ensuring that your work is safe and accessible even if you lose or damage your device.
- **Access Across Devices:** With a reMarkable account, you can access your notes on your computer (via the desktop app) and your smartphone or tablet (via the mobile app). This seamless syncing allows you to continue your work wherever you are.
- **Software Updates:** While the reMarkable 2 receives software updates over Wi-Fi, having an account ensures that these updates are properly associated with your device and that you receive important notifications.
- **Future Features and Services:** reMarkable may introduce new features and services that require a reMarkable account for access.

Creating a reMarkable Account During Initial Setup:

The most common time to create a reMarkable account is during the initial setup of your device. Here's a detailed breakdown:

1. **Account Creation Screen:** After connecting to Wi-Fi during the initial setup, you'll be presented with a screen prompting you to either "Sign in" or "Create account."

2. **Selecting "Create account" (What to Press):**

    ○ Use your Marker to tap on the "Create account" button.
3. **Entering Your Information (What to Press):**

    ○ **Email Address:** A text input field will appear. Use the on-screen keyboard to enter a valid email address that you have access to. This email address will be your username for your reMarkable account. Tap the checkmark or "Next" button on the keyboard to proceed.
    ○ **Password:** You'll be prompted to create a password. Use the on-screen keyboard to enter your desired password. It's crucial to choose a strong password that is difficult for others to guess. A strong password should:

- Be at least 8 characters long.
- Include a mix of uppercase and lowercase letters.
- Include numbers and symbols.
- Avoid easily guessable information like your name, birthday, or common words.
  - **Confirm Password:** You'll be asked to re-enter your password to confirm it. This helps prevent typos.
  - Tap the checkmark or "Next" button on the keyboard to proceed.
4. **Terms and Conditions (What to Press):**

   - You'll be presented with the reMarkable Terms and Conditions and Privacy Policy. It's important to read these documents carefully.
   -
   - If you agree to the terms, tap the "Accept" button.
5. **Account Creation Confirmation:** Once you've accepted the terms, your reMarkable account will be created. You may see a brief message confirming the successful creation of your account.

Creating a reMarkable Account After Initial Setup:

If you skipped account creation during the initial setup or need to create an account later, you can do so through the reMarkable website:

1. **Open a Web Browser:** On your computer or smartphone, open a web browser.

2. **Visit the reMarkable Website:** Go to the reMarkable website (remarkable.com).

3. **Find the Account Creation Page:** Look for a "Sign in" or "Account" link, usually located in the top right corner of the website. Click on it. Then find a "Create Account" or "Sign Up" link.

4. **Follow the On-Screen Instructions:** You'll be guided through the same process as described above: entering your email address, creating a password, and accepting the terms and conditions.

Managing Your reMarkable Account:

Once you have created your reMarkable account, you can manage it through the reMarkable website:

1. **Sign in to Your Account:** Go to the reMarkable website and sign in using your email address and password.

2. **Account Settings:** You'll find options to:

   o **Change your password:** It's a good security practice to change your password periodically.
   o **Manage connected devices:** You can see a list of devices connected to your account.
   o **Manage your subscription (if applicable):** If reMarkable introduces subscription services, you would manage them here.
   o
   o **View billing information (if applicable).**

Troubleshooting Account Creation Issues:

- **Email Address Already in Use:** If you try to create an account with an email address that is already associated with a reMarkable account, you'll see an error message. If you've forgotten your password, use the "Forgot password" option on the sign-in page.
- **Password Issues:** Ensure that your password meets the required criteria (length, complexity, etc.). If you're having trouble remembering your password, use a password manager or write it down in a secure location.
- **Connection Problems:** If you're having trouble connecting to the reMarkable servers during account creation, check your internet connection.

Connecting Your reMarkable 2 to Your Account:

After creating your account (either during setup or through the website), you'll need to connect your reMarkable 2 to it. This happens automatically during initial setup. If for some reason your device isn't connected to your account follow these steps:

1. Access the settings menu by swiping down from the top of the screen and tapping the gear icon.
2. Tap on "Account".
3. If you are not signed in, there will be an option to sign in. Tap it.
4. Enter your reMarkable account email and password using the on-screen keyboard.
5. Tap the checkmark or "Sign in" button.

By creating a reMarkable account, you gain access to the full ecosystem of reMarkable services, ensuring that your work is safe, accessible, and seamlessly synced across your devices. This is a crucial step in maximizing your reMarkable 2 experience.

● *Navigating the interface*

The main screen, often referred to as "My Files," is your home base on the reMarkable 2. It displays your notebooks, folders, PDFs, and other documents.

- **List View:** By default, your files are displayed in a list view. This shows a vertical list of your files with their names and icons.
- **Grid View (What to Press):** You can switch to a grid view by tapping the small icon that looks like four squares in the top right corner of the screen. This displays your files as larger thumbnails, which can be useful for visual browsing. Tap the icon again to return to List View.
- **Sorting Files (What to Press):** You can sort your files by name, date modified, or date created. Tap the three vertical dots icon (More options) in the top right corner and select your preferred sorting method.
- **Searching Files (What to Press):** To search for a specific file, tap the magnifying glass icon in the top bar. Use the on-screen keyboard to enter your search terms.

Opening a File (What to Press):

To open a notebook, PDF, or other document, simply tap on it with your Marker.

Creating a New Notebook or Folder (What to Press):

- **New Notebook:** Tap the "+" button in the top bar and select "New notebook". You'll then be able to choose a template for your notebook.
- **New Folder:** Tap the "+" button and select "New folder". You'll then be prompted to give your folder a name using the on-screen keyboard.

Moving and Organizing Files (What to Press):

- **Selecting Files:** To move or organize files, you first need to select them. Tap and hold on a file icon until a small checkmark appears. You can then tap other files to select multiple items.
- **Moving Files to a Folder:** Once you've selected the files, tap the three vertical dots icon (More options) in the top bar and select "Move". Then choose the destination folder.
- **Deleting Files (What to Press):** After selecting files, tap the trash can icon in the top bar to delete them. You will be asked to confirm the deletion.

The Toolbar (Inside a Notebook or Document):

When you open a notebook or document, a toolbar appears at the top of the screen. This toolbar contains the tools you'll use for writing, drawing, and annotating.

- **Tool Selection (What to Press):** Tap on an icon in the toolbar to select a tool.

- **Pen Tool:** Used for writing and drawing with varying line thickness. Tap the pen icon again to choose different pen types (ballpoint, fineliner, etc.) and adjust the thickness and color.
- **Marker Tool:** Used for highlighting and creating broader strokes. Tap the marker icon again to adjust the thickness and color.
- **Pencil Tool:** Simulates the feel of a traditional pencil. Tap the pencil icon again to adjust the thickness.
- **Eraser Tool:** Used for erasing your strokes. Tap the eraser icon again to choose between a standard eraser and a stroke eraser (which erases entire strokes with one tap).
- **Selection Tool (Lasso):** Used for selecting and moving or deleting parts of your notes.
- **Undo/Redo Arrows (What to Press):** The curved arrows on the toolbar allow you to undo and redo your actions.
- **Layers Tool (What to Press):** The layers icon (looks like stacked sheets of paper) allows you to work with multiple layers in your notes, which can be useful for complex drawings or annotations.
- **Zoom Tool (What to Press):** Tap the magnifying glass icon to zoom in or out of your document. You can also use pinch-to-zoom gestures.
- **More Options (Three Vertical Dots) (What to Press):** This menu contains additional options, such as exporting your document, changing the template, or clearing the page.

Gestures:

The reMarkable 2 supports several intuitive gestures:

- **Writing and Drawing:** Use your Marker directly on the screen to write and draw.
- **Erasing:** If you have the Marker Plus, you can use the eraser end to erase. Otherwise, select the eraser tool from the toolbar.
- **Pinch-to-Zoom:** Use two fingers to pinch in or out to zoom in or out of a document.
- **Two-Finger Pan:** Use two fingers to drag the page around when zoomed in.
- **Swiping Down from the Top:** This opens the quick settings menu, which provides access to Wi-Fi settings, brightness control, and other options.

The Quick Settings Menu (What to Press):

Swiping down from the top of the screen reveals the quick settings menu. This provides quick access to:

- **Wi-Fi:** Turn Wi-Fi on or off and access Wi-Fi settings.
- **Brightness:** Adjust the screen brightness.
- **Rotation Lock:** Lock the screen orientation.
- **Settings (Gear Icon):** Access the full settings menu.

The Settings Menu (What to Press):

The full settings menu can be accessed by tapping the gear icon in the quick settings menu. The settings menu contains options for:

- **Wi-Fi:** Manage Wi-Fi connections.
- **Account:** Manage your reMarkable account.
- **Storage:** View storage usage.
- **Battery:** View battery information.
- **Display:** Adjust display settings.
- **Handwriting conversion:** Configure handwriting conversion settings.
- **About:** View device information and software version.

By mastering these navigation techniques, you'll be able to efficiently navigate the reMarkable 2's interface and take full advantage of its features. This intuitive design combined with the paper-like feel creates a truly unique and productive digital experience.

Basic gestures and controls

The reMarkable 2's user interface is designed to be intuitive and mimic the experience of using pen and paper. This section provides a comprehensive guide to the basic gestures and controls that will allow you to interact with your device effectively.

1. Writing and Drawing:

- **The Marker:** The primary input method for the reMarkable 2 is the Marker (or Marker Plus). It's designed to feel like a real pen or pencil on paper.
- **Applying Pressure:** The reMarkable 2 is pressure-sensitive. Applying more pressure will create thicker, darker lines, while lighter pressure will result in thinner, lighter lines. This allows for expressive writing and drawing.
- **Angle Sensitivity (Tilt Support - Marker Plus):** The Marker Plus supports tilt sensitivity. Changing the angle of the Marker Plus allows for shading and varied line widths, similar to using a real pencil or brush. This feature is not available with the standard Marker.

2. Erasing:

- **Using the Eraser (Marker Plus):** The Marker Plus has an eraser on the back end. Simply flip the Marker Plus over and use the eraser on the screen to erase your strokes.
- **Using the Eraser Tool (Both Markers):** If you have the standard Marker or prefer using the on-screen tool, tap the eraser icon in the toolbar. You can then erase by dragging the Marker over the area you want to erase.
- **Stroke Eraser (Eraser Tool Option):** Within the eraser tool options (tap the eraser icon again), you can choose the stroke eraser. This will erase entire strokes with a single tap, rather than requiring you to drag the eraser.

3. Navigation Gestures:

- **Tapping:** A single tap with the Marker is used to select items, open files, activate tools, and interact with on-screen buttons.
- **Swiping:**
  - **Swiping Down from the Top:** This gesture opens the quick settings menu, providing access to Wi-Fi, brightness, rotation lock, and settings.
  - **Swiping Pages (in Notebooks/PDFs):** In a notebook or PDF, swipe left or right to turn pages.
- **Tap and Hold (Long Press):** Tapping and holding on an item (like a notebook or file) will select it for actions like moving, deleting, or duplicating. This is also used to access contextual menus in some cases.
- **Pinch-to-Zoom:** Using two fingers, pinch inwards on the screen to zoom out and pinch outwards to zoom in. This is useful for viewing details in drawings or PDFs.
- **Two-Finger Pan (Drag):** When zoomed in, use two fingers to drag the page around to view different parts of the document.

4. Toolbar Interactions:

- **Selecting Tools (What to Press):** Tap on an icon in the toolbar to select a tool (pen, marker, eraser, etc.).
- **Tool Options (What to Press):** Tapping on a selected tool icon again will usually open a menu with options for that tool, such as changing pen type, thickness, color, or eraser type.
- **Undo/Redo (What to Press):** The curved arrow icons in the toolbar are for undoing and redoing actions. Tap the left arrow to undo the last action, and tap the right arrow to redo an undone action.

5. On-Screen Keyboard:

- **Activating the Keyboard:** The on-screen keyboard appears automatically when you need to enter text, such as when naming a new notebook or folder, searching for a file, or entering a Wi-Fi password.
- **Using the Keyboard (What to Press):** Use your Marker to tap on the keys to enter text. The keyboard includes:
    - **Letters:** Standard QWERTY layout.
    - **Numbers and Symbols:** Accessible by tapping the "123" or "?123" key.
    - **Shift Key:** Used to type uppercase letters or access alternate symbols.
    - **Backspace Key:** Used to delete the last entered character.
    - **Enter/Return Key:** Used to confirm text input or move to the next line.

6. Contextual Menus:

In some situations, tapping the three vertical dots icon (More options) will open a contextual menu with actions specific to the current context. For example:

- **In the "My Files" view:** The More options menu allows you to sort files, create new folders, or access global settings.
- **Inside a notebook:** The More options menu may include options for exporting the notebook, changing the template, or clearing the page.

7. Quick Settings Menu:

- **Accessing the Quick Settings (What to Press):** Swipe down from the top of the screen to access the quick settings menu.
- **Quick Settings Options (What to Press):** This menu provides quick access to:
    - **Wi-Fi:** Toggle Wi-Fi on/off and access Wi-Fi settings.
    - **Brightness:** Adjust the screen brightness.
    - **Rotation Lock:** Lock the screen orientation.
    - **Settings (Gear Icon):** Access the full settings menu.

Tips for Using Gestures and Controls:

- **Practice:** The best way to become comfortable with the reMarkable 2's gestures and controls is to practice using them. Try creating a new notebook and experimenting with the different tools and gestures.
- **Light Touch:** A light touch is generally sufficient for most interactions. You don't need to press hard on the screen.
- **Clean Screen:** A clean screen will ensure optimal Marker tracking and prevent accidental inputs.

The reMarkable 2's interface is designed for simplicity and focus, and the toolbar and menus play a key role in achieving this. This section provides a detailed breakdown of the toolbar and menus you'll encounter while using your reMarkable 2, explaining the function of each icon and option.

I. The Toolbar (Within a Notebook or Document):

The toolbar appears at the top of the screen when you open a notebook, PDF, or other document. It provides quick access to the tools you'll use for writing, drawing, annotating, and managing your content.

- **1. Pen Tool (What to Press):**

    o **Icon:** A pen nib.
    o **Function:** Used for general writing and drawing.
    o **Options (Tap the icon again):** Tapping the pen icon again opens a menu with options to:
        ▪ **Change Pen Type:** Choose from various pen types like ballpoint, fineliner, marker, and calligraphy pen, each with different line characteristics.
        ▪ **Adjust Thickness:** Select from predefined thickness options or use the slider for finer control.
        ▪ **Change Color:** Choose from a limited but effective palette of colors (black, gray, white, and sometimes other colors depending on software updates).
- **2. Marker Tool (What to Press):**

    o **Icon:** A marker tip.
    o **Function:** Used for highlighting and creating broader strokes.
    o **Options (Tap the icon again):** Similar to the pen tool, tapping the marker icon again allows you to adjust thickness and color.
- **3. Pencil Tool (What to Press):**

    o **Icon:** A pencil tip.
    o **Function:** Simulates the feel of a traditional pencil, with varying levels of shading depending on pressure.
    o **Options (Tap the icon again):** You can adjust the thickness of the pencil line.

- **4. Eraser Tool (What to Press):**

  - **Icon:** An eraser.
  - **Function:** Used for erasing your strokes.
  - **Options (Tap the icon again):**
    - **Standard Eraser:** Erases by dragging the eraser over the area you want to remove.
    - **Stroke Eraser:** Erases entire strokes with a single tap.
- **5. Selection Tool (Lasso) (What to Press):**

  - **Icon:** A lasso.
  - **Function:** Used for selecting specific parts of your notes or drawings. Once selected, you can move, resize, cut, copy, or delete the selected area.
  - **How to Use:** Draw a freehand loop around the content you wish to select.
- **6. Undo/Redo Arrows (What to Press):**

  - **Icons:** Curved arrows pointing left (undo) and right (redo).
  - **Function:** Undo reverses your last action, while Redo reapplies an undone action.
- **7. Layers Tool (What to Press):**

  - **Icon:** Stacked sheets of paper.
  - **Function:** Allows you to work with multiple layers in your notes. This is useful for complex drawings or annotations, as you can draw on separate layers without affecting other parts of your work.
  - **Options (Tap the icon):** Opens a menu to manage layers: add new layers, delete layers, hide/show layers, and reorder layers.
- **8. Zoom Tool (What to Press):**

  - **Icon:** A magnifying glass.
  - **Function:** Allows you to zoom in and out of your document for more detailed work or a broader overview.
  - **How to Use:** Tap the icon, and then use pinch-to-zoom gestures on the screen.
- **9. More Options (Three Vertical Dots) (What to Press):**

  - **Icon:** Three vertical dots.
  - **Function:** This menu contains additional options specific to the current context (within a notebook or document). Common options include:
    - **Export:** Export your document as a PDF, PNG, or SVG file.

- **Change Template:** Change the background template of your notebook page.
- **Clear Page:** Erase all content on the current page.
- **Convert to text:** Convert your handwritten notes to typed text (if handwriting recognition is enabled).
- **Copy Page:** Duplicate the current page.
- **Move Page:** Move the current page to a different location within the notebook.

II. The Quick Settings Menu (Swipe Down from Top):

Swiping down from the top of the screen reveals the quick settings menu. This provides quick access to frequently used settings.

- **Wi-Fi (What to Press):**

  - **Function:** Toggle Wi-Fi on or off and access Wi-Fi settings to connect to different networks or manage saved networks.
- **Brightness (What to Press):**

  - **Function:** Adjust the screen brightness using a slider.
- **Rotation Lock (What to Press):**

  - **Function:** Lock the screen orientation in either portrait or landscape mode.
- **Settings (Gear Icon) (What to Press):**

  - **Function:** Opens the full settings menu.

III. The Settings Menu (Accessed via Quick Settings):

The full settings menu provides access to more advanced settings and configurations.

- **Wi-Fi:** Manage Wi-Fi connections.
- **Account:** Manage your reMarkable account, including signing in/out.
- **Storage:** View storage usage on your device.
- **Battery:** View battery information and manage power settings.
- **Display:** Adjust display settings, such as dark mode.
- **Handwriting conversion:** Configure handwriting conversion settings, such as supported languages.
- **About:** View device information, software version, and legal information.

IV. Contextual Menus (Tap the Three Vertical Dots in Different Contexts):

The three vertical dots icon (More options) appears in various contexts throughout the reMarkable 2 interface and offers context-specific options.

- **In "My Files" View:**

  - **Sort:** Sort files by name, date modified, or date created.
  - **New Folder:** Create a new folder to organize your files.
  - **Select All:** Select all files in the current view.
- **When a File is Selected (in "My Files"):**

  - **Move:** Move the selected file(s) to a different folder.
  - **Duplicate:** Create a copy of the selected file(s).
  - **Delete:** Delete the selected file(s).

Understanding the toolbar and menus is fundamental to efficiently using your reMarkable 2. By familiarizing yourself with these controls, you can streamline your workflow and focus on what matters most: your ideas and your work.

CHAPTER 2

<u>The Basics of Note-Taking</u>

The Basics of Note-Taking dives into the core functionality of the reMarkable 2: creating and managing digital notes. This chapter will guide you through the process of creating your first notebook, selecting from a variety of templates and covers to suit your needs, and mastering the different writing tools available. We'll explore how to adjust stroke thickness and color to personalize your notes, as well as how to effectively erase mistakes and undo actions. Finally, we'll introduce you to the concepts of inserting and manipulating shapes and working with layers, providing you with the foundational skills to create organized and visually appealing digital notes. By the end of this chapter, you'll be well-equipped to use the reMarkable 2 as your primary tool for note-taking, brainstorming, and creative expression.

Creating your first notebook

Creating notebooks is the fundamental action on the reMarkable 2, serving as the digital equivalent of starting a new physical notebook. This guide provides a comprehensive walkthrough of creating your first notebook, exploring the various templates and covers available, and understanding how these choices impact your note-taking experience.

1. Accessing the "My Files" Screen:

The "My Files" screen is your central hub for managing all your notebooks, folders, and documents. If you're not already there, you'll arrive here upon powering on the device.

2. Initiating Notebook Creation (What to Press):

- **The "+" Button:** Locate the "+" button in the top bar of the "My Files" screen. This button initiates the creation of new items.
- **Tap the "+" Button:** Use your Marker to tap the "+" button.

3. Choosing "New notebook" (What to Press):

- **The Creation Menu:** After tapping the "+", a small menu will appear with two options: "New notebook" and "New folder."
- **Tap "New notebook":** Use your Marker to tap on "New notebook." This will open the notebook creation interface.

4. Selecting a Template:

The template you choose determines the background of your notebook pages. The reMarkable 2 offers a diverse range of templates to cater to various needs.

- **Template Categories:** The templates are organized into categories, making it easier to find the right one for your purpose. Common categories include:

  - **Lined:** Standard lined paper for general note-taking.
  - **Grid:** Grid paper for diagrams, graphs, and technical drawings.
  - **Dotted:** Dotted paper for bullet journaling, sketching, and flexible layouts.
  - **Blank:** A completely blank canvas for freehand drawing and creative work.
  - **Planner:** Templates designed for daily, weekly, or monthly planning.
  - **Specialized:** Templates for specific tasks like music notation, storyboarding, or meeting minutes.
- **Browsing Templates (What to Press):**

  - **Scrolling:** Use your Marker to swipe up or down on the template list to browse through the available options.
  - **Category Tabs (If available):** Some software versions organize templates into tabs at the top for faster navigation. Tap on a tab to view templates within that category.
- **Selecting a Template (What to Press):** Once you find a template you like, tap on it with your Marker to select it.

5. Choosing a Cover:

The cover you choose appears as the thumbnail for your notebook in the "My Files" view, providing a visual way to distinguish your notebooks.

- **Cover Options:** The reMarkable 2 offers a selection of cover designs, ranging from simple solid colors to more elaborate patterns and textures.

- **Browsing Covers (What to Press):**

  - **Swiping:** Swipe left or right on the cover previews to browse through the available options.
- **Selecting a Cover (What to Press):** Tap on the cover you want to use.

6. Naming Your Notebook (What to Press):

- **On-Screen Keyboard:** After selecting a template and cover, the on-screen keyboard will appear.
- **Typing the Name:** Use your Marker to tap on the keys to type the name of your notebook.
- **Confirming the Name (What to Press):** Tap the checkmark or "Done" button on the keyboard to confirm the name.

7. Creating the Notebook (What to Press):

- **The "Create" Button (What to Press):** After naming your notebook, a "Create" button will appear in the bottom right corner of the screen.
- **Tap "Create":** Use your Marker to tap the "Create" button. This will create your new notebook and open it, ready for you to start taking notes.

Example Scenarios for Template Selection:

- **For General Note-Taking:** The "Lined" template is a classic choice for taking notes in meetings, lectures, or during brainstorming sessions.
- **For Sketching and Drawing:** The "Blank" template provides a completely free canvas for artistic expression. The "Dotted" template can also be useful for sketching, offering subtle guidance without being as restrictive as a grid.
- **For Technical Drawings or Diagrams:** The "Grid" template is ideal for creating precise diagrams, graphs, and technical drawings.
- **For Planning and Organization:** The "Planner" templates offer various layouts for daily, weekly, or monthly planning, helping you stay organized and manage your time effectively.

Managing Existing Notebooks:

- **Renaming a Notebook (What to Press):**

  1. In "My Files," tap and hold on the notebook you want to rename.
  2. Tap the three vertical dots icon (More options).
  3. Select "Rename".
  4. Use the on-screen keyboard to enter the new name and tap the checkmark.
- **Deleting a Notebook (What to Press):**

  1. In "My Files," tap and hold on the notebook you want to delete.
  2. Tap the trash can icon in the top bar.
  3. Confirm the deletion.
- **Duplicating a Notebook (What to Press):**

1. In "My Files," tap and hold on the notebook you want to duplicate.
2. Tap the three vertical dots icon (More options).
3. Select "Duplicate".

Tips for Organizing Your Notebooks:

- **Use Descriptive Names:** Give your notebooks clear and descriptive names that reflect their content. This will make it easier to find them later.
- **Use Folders:** Create folders to organize your notebooks into categories, such as "Work," "Personal," "Projects," or "Courses."
- **Regularly Review and Archive:** Periodically review your notebooks and archive or delete any that are no longer needed.

By following these steps, you can easily create and manage your notebooks on the reMarkable 2, tailoring them to your specific needs and preferences. This digital notebook system provides a flexible and organized way to capture your thoughts, ideas, and information.

• *Choosing templates and covers*

Templates and covers are essential elements for personalizing your digital notebooks on the reMarkable 2. Templates provide the background layout for your pages, while covers offer a visual identifier for your notebooks in the "My Files" view. This comprehensive guide explores the available templates and covers, explaining their uses and guiding you through the selection process.

I. Understanding Templates:

Templates define the underlying structure of your notebook pages. They offer different layouts and guidelines to suit various note-taking, sketching, and planning needs.

Template Categories and Examples:

The reMarkable 2 organizes templates into categories, making it easier to find the right one. These categories may vary slightly depending on software updates, but common ones include:

- **Lined:**

  - **Narrow Lined:** Closely spaced lines for detailed writing.
  - **Wide Lined:** Widely spaced lines for larger handwriting or note-taking with more space.

- **College Ruled:** A standard line spacing commonly used in college notebooks.
- **Legal Ruled:** Wider spacing than college ruled, often used for legal documents.
- **Use Cases:** General note-taking, writing, journaling.

- **Grid:**

  - **Small Grid:** Closely spaced grid lines for precise drawings and diagrams.
  - **Large Grid:** Widely spaced grid lines for larger diagrams or sketching.
  - **Isometric Grid:** A grid with angled lines, useful for 3D drawings and perspective sketches.
  - **Use Cases:** Technical drawings, diagrams, graphs, architectural sketches, pixel art.

- **Dotted:**

  - **Small Dots:** Closely spaced dots for subtle guidance while sketching or writing.
  - **Large Dots:** Widely spaced dots for more open layouts and bullet journaling.
  - **Use Cases:** Sketching, bullet journaling, mind mapping, freehand writing with subtle guidance.

- **Blank:**

  - **Blank Canvas:** A completely empty page with no lines, grids, or dots.
  - **Use Cases:** Freehand drawing, sketching, brainstorming, mind mapping without any constraints.

- **Planner:**

  - **Daily Planner:** Layouts for daily scheduling and task management.
  - **Weekly Planner:** Layouts for weekly overviews and appointments.
  - **Monthly Planner:** Layouts for monthly planning and goal setting.
  - **Use Cases:** Time management, scheduling, task tracking, appointment planning.

- **Specialized:**

  - **Music Paper:** Staff lines for writing music.
  - **Storyboards:** Templates with frames for visualizing scenes.
  - **Meeting Minutes:** Templates with sections for recording meeting notes, action items, and attendees.
  - **Use Cases:** Specific professional or creative tasks.

II. Choosing a Template (What to Press):

You choose a template when creating a new notebook or when changing the template of an existing page.

- **Creating a New Notebook:**

    1. **Tap the "+" button** on the "My Files" screen.
    2. **Tap "New notebook."**
    3. The template selection screen will appear.
    4. **Swipe up or down** to browse the template categories and templates within each category.
    5. **Tap on the desired template** to select it.
- **Changing the Template of an Existing Page:**

    1. **Open the notebook** containing the page you want to change.
    2. **Tap the three vertical dots icon (More options)** in the toolbar.
    3. **Tap "Change template."**
    4. The template selection screen will appear.
    5. **Swipe up or down** to browse the available templates.
    6. **Tap on the desired template** to apply it to the current page.

III. Understanding Covers:

Covers provide a visual representation of your notebooks in the "My Files" view. They help you quickly identify and differentiate between your various notebooks.

Cover Styles:

The reMarkable 2 offers a variety of cover styles, including:

- **Solid Colors:** Simple covers with a single color.
- **Patterns:** Covers with various patterns and textures.
- **Minimalist Designs:** Clean and simple designs with subtle details.

IV. Choosing a Cover (What to Press):

You choose a cover when creating a new notebook.

- **Creating a New Notebook:**
    1. **Tap the "+" button** on the "My Files" screen.
    2. **Tap "New notebook."**
    3. After selecting a template, the cover selection screen will appear.

4. **Swipe left or right** to browse the available covers.
5. **Tap on the desired cover** to select it.

V. Best Practices for Choosing Templates and Covers:

- **Choose Templates Based on Purpose:** Select a template that best suits the type of notes or work you'll be doing. For example, use lined paper for general notes, grid paper for diagrams, and blank paper for freehand drawing.
- **Use Covers for Organization:** Use different covers to visually categorize your notebooks. For example, you could use different colors for different subjects or projects.
- **Experiment and Find Your Preferences:** Don't be afraid to experiment with different templates and covers to find what works best for you.
- **Consider Dark Mode:** If you use dark mode on your reMarkable 2, consider how the templates and covers will look in this mode. Some templates may be better suited for dark mode than others.

VI. No Custom Covers:

It is important to note that, as of the current software version, the reMarkable 2 does *not* support custom covers. You are limited to the pre-installed options.

VII. Template Updates:

reMarkable occasionally adds new templates through software updates. Ensure your device is updated to access the latest options.

By carefully selecting templates and covers, you can personalize your reMarkable 2 experience and create a digital notebook system that is both functional and visually appealing. This personalization enhances your workflow and makes using your reMarkable 2 even more enjoyable.

Using the different writing tools (pens, markers, pencils)

The reMarkable 2's writing experience is designed to mimic the feel of pen on paper, and the various writing tools available play a crucial role in achieving this. This comprehensive guide will delve into the different writing tools—pens, markers, and pencils—explaining their unique characteristics, how to adjust their settings, and providing tips for optimal use.

I. Accessing the Writing Tools (What to Press):

When you open a notebook or document on your reMarkable 2, the toolbar appears at the top of the screen. The writing tools are located on this toolbar.

- **Tapping a Tool Icon:** To select a writing tool, simply tap its icon with your Marker. The selected tool will be highlighted.

II. The Pen Tool:

The pen tool is the most versatile writing tool on the reMarkable 2, suitable for general note-taking, writing, and detailed drawing.

- **Icon:** A pen nib.

- **Characteristics:** Creates consistent lines with varying thickness based on pressure.

- **Pen Types (What to Press):** Tapping the pen icon again opens a menu with different pen types:

  - **Ballpoint Pen:** Creates a smooth, consistent line similar to a ballpoint pen.
  - **Fineliner:** Creates a thin, precise line, ideal for detailed work and fine writing.
  - **Marker Pen:** Creates a thicker, more pronounced line, similar to a felt-tip marker.
  - **Calligraphy Pen:** Creates lines that vary in thickness depending on the angle and pressure of the Marker, mimicking the effect of a calligraphy pen.
- **Adjusting Thickness (What to Press):** Within the pen options menu, you can adjust the thickness of the line.

  - **Predefined Thicknesses:** Several preset thickness options are available (e.g., thin, medium, thick). Tap on one to select it.
  - **Thickness Slider:** A slider provides finer control over the line thickness. Drag the slider to the left for thinner lines and to the right for thicker lines.
- **Adjusting Color (What to Press):** Within the pen options menu, you can select the color of the ink. The available color palette is intentionally limited to encourage focus and avoid distractions. The standard options are black, grey, and white. Some software updates may include additional colours. Tap on the desired color to select it.

III. The Marker Tool:

The marker tool is designed for highlighting, underlining, and creating broad strokes.

- **Icon:** A marker tip.
- **Characteristics:** Creates broad, semi-transparent strokes. The intensity of the color depends on the pressure applied.
- **Adjusting Thickness (What to Press):** Similar to the pen tool, tapping the marker icon again allows you to adjust the thickness of the marker stroke using predefined options or a slider.
- **Adjusting Color (What to Press):** You can also change the color of the marker ink within the marker options menu.

IV. The Pencil Tool:

The pencil tool simulates the feel of a traditional graphite pencil, with varying levels of shading depending on pressure.

- **Icon:** A pencil tip.
- **Characteristics:** Creates textured lines that vary in darkness and thickness depending on pressure. Applying more pressure creates darker, thicker lines, while lighter pressure creates lighter, thinner lines.
- **Adjusting Thickness (What to Press):** Tapping the pencil icon again allows you to adjust the thickness of the pencil line. Unlike the pen and marker, the pencil tool doesn't offer colour options.

V. Using the Tools Effectively:

- **Pressure Sensitivity:** Experiment with different levels of pressure to see how it affects the line thickness and darkness for each tool. This is key to achieving expressive writing and drawing.
- **Angle Sensitivity (Marker Plus Only):** If you have the Marker Plus, experiment with tilting the Marker to see how it affects the line width and shading, especially with the calligraphy pen and pencil tools.
- **Combining Tools:** Use different tools in combination to create interesting effects. For example, you could use the pen tool for writing notes, the marker tool for highlighting key points, and the pencil tool for sketching diagrams.
- **Tool Presets:** While the reMarkable 2 doesn't offer explicit tool presets in the traditional sense, remembering your preferred thickness and color settings for each tool allows you to quickly switch between your go-to configurations.

VI. Troubleshooting Common Issues:

- **No Ink/Lines Appearing:** Ensure that your Marker is properly connected to the reMarkable 2 and that the nib is not damaged. Try replacing the nib if necessary.
- **Inconsistent Lines:** Check the nib of your Marker for wear and tear. A worn nib can cause inconsistent lines. Also, ensure the screen is clean.
- **Marker Not Responding:** Try restarting your reMarkable 2.

VII. Tips and Tricks:

- **Practice Strokes:** Practice drawing different types of lines and shapes with each tool to get a feel for their characteristics.
- **Use Layers for Complex Drawings:** When creating complex drawings, use layers to separate different elements. This will make it easier to edit and manipulate individual parts of your drawing.
- **Experiment with Different Templates:** The type of template you choose can also affect the writing experience. For example, lined paper can provide guidance for writing straight lines, while blank paper allows for more freedom in sketching and drawing.

By understanding the unique characteristics of each writing tool and practicing their use, you can unlock the full potential of the reMarkable 2 for note-taking, sketching, and creative expression. The combination of pressure sensitivity, different pen types, and the paper-like feel of the device creates a truly unique and enjoyable digital writing experience.

- *Adjusting stroke thickness and color*

The ability to adjust stroke thickness and color is essential for creating expressive and organized notes on the reMarkable 2.

I. Accessing Tool Options (What to Press):

Before you can adjust stroke thickness or color, you need to select a writing tool and then access its options menu.

1. **Select a Tool:** Tap on the icon of the desired writing tool (pen, marker, or pencil) in the toolbar.
2.
3. **Open the Options Menu:** Tap the same tool icon again. This will open the tool's options menu.

II. Adjusting Stroke Thickness:

The way you adjust thickness varies slightly depending on the tool.

A. Pen and Marker:

1. **Predefined Thicknesses (What to Press):** In the pen or marker options menu, you'll see several preset thickness options, often represented by circles of varying sizes (e.g., thin, medium, thick). Tap on one of these circles to quickly select a predefined thickness.

2. **Thickness Slider (What to Press):** For finer control, use the thickness slider.

   o **Drag the Slider:** Use your Marker to drag the slider left to decrease the thickness or right to increase it.

B. Pencil:

The pencil tool typically only offers predefined thickness options.

1. **Predefined Thicknesses (What to Press):** In the pencil options menu, you'll see a few preset thickness options. Tap on one to select it.

III. Adjusting Color:

The reMarkable 2 offers a limited but effective color palette.

1. **Color Palette (What to Press):** In the pen or marker options menu, you'll see the available colors. The standard options are black, gray, and white. Some software updates may introduce additional colors, especially for export purposes (e.g., highlighting in color for exported PDFs).
2.
3. **Selecting a Color (What to Press):** Tap on the desired color to select it.

IV. Specific Tool Behaviors:

- **Pen:** The pen tool's line weight is highly responsive to pressure. Even with a set thickness, applying more pressure will result in a slightly thicker and darker line.
- **Marker:** The marker tool creates semi-transparent strokes. Overlapping strokes will result in a darker shade. The thickness and opacity are also affected by pressure.
- **Pencil:** The pencil tool simulates graphite, with shading effects based on pressure and tilt (if you have the Marker Plus). The thickness options control the overall width of the "lead."

V. Practical Applications of Stroke Thickness and Color:

- **Hierarchy and Emphasis:** Use thicker strokes for headings and key points, and thinner strokes for supporting details. Use color to highlight important information or categorize different sections of your notes.
- **Visual Organization:** Use different colors for different topics or categories of information. This can make your notes easier to scan and review.
- **Sketching and Drawing:** Varying stroke thickness and color is essential for creating depth, texture, and visual interest in your sketches and drawings.
- **Annotations:** Use different colors for different types of annotations, such as highlighting, underlining, or adding comments.

VI. Remembering Your Preferences:

The reMarkable 2 remembers the last used thickness and color for each tool. This allows you to quickly switch between your preferred settings without having to readjust them each time.

VII. Tips and Tricks:

- **Experiment:** The best way to understand how stroke thickness and color work is to experiment with different settings and see how they affect your writing and drawing.
- **Use Layers (for Complex Work):** If you're creating complex drawings or annotations, use layers to separate different elements. This will make it easier to edit and adjust individual parts without affecting others.
- **Consider Exporting:** Remember that the on-screen colors (especially for highlighting) may appear as shades of gray on the reMarkable 2's monochrome display but will be exported in their respective colors (if the feature is supported for that tool).

By mastering the adjustment of stroke thickness and color, you can significantly enhance the clarity, organization, and visual appeal of your notes and drawings on the reMarkable 2. This level of control allows for a truly personalized and effective digital writing experience.

• *Erasing and undoing mistakes*

Making mistakes is a natural part of the creative process, and the reMarkable 2 provides several ways to correct them, ensuring a smooth and frustration-free experience. This guide will cover the different erasing methods and the undo/redo functionality, empowering you to confidently create and refine your work.

I. Erasing Methods:

The reMarkable 2 offers two primary ways to erase: using the eraser end of the Marker Plus (if you have one) or using the on-screen eraser tool.

A. Using the Eraser (Marker Plus Only):

If you have the Marker Plus, erasing is as simple as flipping the Marker over.

1. **Flip the Marker:** Simply turn the Marker Plus around so that the eraser end is facing the screen.
2. **Erase:** Use the eraser end just like you would a traditional eraser on paper. Rub it over the strokes you want to remove.

B. Using the Eraser Tool (Both Markers):

Both the standard Marker and the Marker Plus can use the on-screen eraser tool.

1. **Select the Eraser Tool (What to Press):** Tap the eraser icon in the toolbar.
2. **Erase:** Drag the Marker over the strokes you want to erase.

Eraser Tool Options (What to Press):

Tapping the eraser icon again opens a menu with different erasing modes:

- **Standard Eraser:** This is the default mode. It erases the area you rub with the Marker.
- **Stroke Eraser:** This mode erases entire strokes with a single tap. If you tap on any part of a stroke, the whole stroke will be erased.

C. Erase All (What to Press):

To clear the entire page, you can use the "Erase all" option.

1. **Access More Options:** Tap the three vertical dots icon (More options) in the toolbar.
2. **Select "Clear Page":** Tap "Clear Page" from the menu. This will erase all content on the current page.

II. Undoing and Redoing Actions:

The reMarkable 2 also provides undo and redo functionality, allowing you to quickly revert or reapply your last actions.

A. Using the Undo/Redo Icons (What to Press):

The toolbar contains dedicated undo and redo icons.

- **Undo:** Tap the left-pointing curved arrow to undo your last action.
- **Redo:** Tap the right-pointing curved arrow to redo an action you've undone.

B. Using Gestures for Undo/Redo:

The reMarkable 2 also supports gestures for undo and redo.

- **Two-Finger Tap for Undo:** Tapping the screen once with two fingers will undo your last action.
- **Three-Finger Tap for Redo:** Tapping the screen once with three fingers will redo an undone action.

III. Important Considerations:

- **What Cannot Be Erased:** You can only erase strokes that you have created with the writing tools (pens, markers, and pencils). You cannot erase:
  - Content from imported PDFs or ebooks.
  - Typed text (if you have converted handwriting to text).
  - Template backgrounds.
- **Precision Erasing:** For precise erasing, zoom in on the area you want to erase using the pinch-to-zoom gesture.
- **Layer Considerations:** If you are working with layers, erasing will only affect the currently active layer.

IV. Tips and Tricks:

- **Use the Stroke Eraser for Efficiency:** The stroke eraser can be a very efficient way to remove entire strokes quickly, especially when working on complex drawings or notes.
- **Combine Erasing and Undo/Redo:** Use a combination of erasing and undo/redo to quickly correct mistakes and refine your work. For example, if you accidentally erase too much, use the redo function to restore it.
- **Practice:** Experiment with the different erasing methods and undo/redo functionality to become comfortable with them.

- *Inserting and manipulating shapes*

While the reMarkable 2 doesn't have a dedicated "shape tool" in the traditional sense (like those found in drawing software), it offers a smart and intuitive way to create basic shapes and manipulate them. This guide explains how to draw and perfect shapes, along with how to manipulate them within your notes.

I. Creating Basic Shapes:

The reMarkable 2 uses a gesture-based approach to create shapes. You draw a rough approximation of the shape you want, and the device automatically perfects it.

1. **Select a Writing Tool:** Choose any of the writing tools (pen, marker, or pencil). The fineliner pen often provides the cleanest results for shape creation.

2. **Draw a Rough Shape:** Draw the shape you want (circle, square, rectangle, triangle, or line) on the screen. Don't worry about making it perfect.

3. **Hold at the End:** Once you've completed the rough shape, hold your Marker still for a brief moment at the point where you finished drawing.

4. **Shape Perfection:** The reMarkable 2 will recognize your intended shape and automatically convert it into a perfect version.

Specific Shape Behaviors:

- **Circles:** Drawing a rough circle and holding will create a perfect circle.
- **Squares/Rectangles:** Drawing a rough square or rectangle and holding will create a perfect square or rectangle. You can influence whether a rectangle or square is created by the proportions of your initial drawing.
- **Triangles:** Drawing a rough triangle and holding will create a triangle with straight lines.
- **Straight Lines:** Drawing a rough line and holding will create a perfectly straight line.

II. Manipulating Shapes:

Once you've created a shape, you can manipulate it using the selection tool.

1. **Select the Selection Tool (Lasso) (What to Press):** Tap the lasso icon in the toolbar.

2. **Select the Shape:** Draw a loop around the shape you want to manipulate. Make sure the entire shape is enclosed within the lasso.

3. **Manipulation Options:** Once the shape is selected, you can perform the following actions:

   - **Moving the Shape (What to Press):** Tap and hold inside the selected shape and drag it to the desired location.
   - **Resizing the Shape (What to Press):** Small circles (handles) will appear at the corners and sides of the selected shape. Tap and drag these handles to resize the shape. Dragging a corner handle will resize the shape proportionally, while dragging a side handle will resize it in only one dimension.
   - **Cutting/Copying/Pasting the Shape (What to Press):** Tap the three vertical dots icon (More options) while the shape is selected. You'll see options for "Cut," "Copy," and "Paste."
     - **Cut:** Removes the shape from its current location and copies it to the clipboard.
     - **Copy:** Copies the shape to the clipboard without removing it from its current location.
     - **Paste:** Pastes a copy of the shape from the clipboard to the current page. You can paste the shape multiple times.
   - **Deleting the Shape (What to Press):** With the shape selected, tap the trash can icon in the toolbar.

III. Combining Shapes:

You can combine multiple shapes to create more complex diagrams or drawings.

1. **Create Multiple Shapes:** Use the shape creation method described above to create several shapes.

2. **Arrange and Overlap:** Use the selection tool to move and overlap the shapes as desired.

IV. Limitations:

- **Limited Shape Recognition:** The reMarkable 2's shape recognition is limited to basic geometric shapes (circles, squares, rectangles, triangles, and lines). It does not recognize more complex shapes or freehand drawings as shapes.
- **No Predefined Shape Library:** There is no library of predefined shapes that you can insert. You must draw each shape manually.
- **No Fill Color:** You cannot fill shapes with color. Only the outline of the shape is created.

V. Tips and Tricks:

- **Practice Drawing Smooth Shapes:** The smoother your initial drawing, the better the shape recognition will be.
- **Use the Zoom Function:** Zooming in can help you create more precise shapes, especially smaller ones.
- **Use Layers for Complex Diagrams:** If you are creating complex diagrams with many shapes, use layers to organize the different elements. This will make it easier to edit and manipulate individual shapes without affecting others.
- **Combine with Other Tools:** Combine shapes with other tools like the pen and marker to add details and annotations to your diagrams.

By understanding how to create and manipulate shapes on the reMarkable 2, you can enhance your note-taking, sketching, and diagramming capabilities. While the shape functionality is not as extensive as dedicated drawing software, it provides a convenient and intuitive way to create basic geometric forms within your notes.

• *Working with layers*

Layers are a powerful feature on the reMarkable 2 that allow you to organize and manage different elements of your notes and drawings independently. Think of layers as transparent sheets of paper stacked on top of each other. You can draw or write on each layer without affecting the content on other layers. This guide explains how to use layers effectively, enhancing your creative workflow.

I. Accessing the Layers Menu (What to Press):

1. **Open a Notebook or Document:** Open the notebook or document where you want to use layers.
2. **Tap the Layers Icon:** Tap the icon that looks like stacked sheets of paper in the toolbar. This will open the Layers menu.

II. Understanding the Layers Menu:

The Layers menu displays a list of the layers in your document.

- **Background Layer:** The bottommost layer is the background layer. This layer contains the template you selected for your notebook page. You cannot delete or move the background layer.

- **Active Layer:** The currently selected layer is the active layer. Any writing or drawing you do will be added to this layer. The active layer is indicated by a highlighted bar or a different color.
- **Layer Visibility:** Each layer has a visibility icon (an eye). Tapping the eye icon toggles the visibility of that layer. When the eye is open, the layer is visible. When the eye is closed, the layer is hidden.

III. Adding a New Layer (What to Press):

1. **Open the Layers Menu:** As described above.
2. **Tap "Add Layer":** Tap the "Add Layer" button (usually a "+" symbol or text) at the bottom of the Layers menu. A new layer will be added above the currently active layer.
3. **Maximum Layers:** The reMarkable 2 supports a limited number of layers (typically five). If you try to add more layers than the maximum allowed, you'll receive a notification.

IV. Selecting a Layer (What to Press):

To make a layer active, simply tap on it in the Layers menu.

V. Hiding and Showing Layers (What to Press):

To hide a layer, tap the eye icon next to its name in the Layers menu. To show a hidden layer, tap the eye icon again.

VI. Reordering Layers (What to Press):

You can change the stacking order of layers.

1. **Open the Layers Menu:** As described above.
2. **Tap and Hold a Layer:** Tap and hold on the layer you want to move.
3. **Drag the Layer:** Drag the layer up or down in the list to change its position.

VII. Merging Layers (What to Press):

You can combine two layers into a single layer.

1. **Open the Layers Menu:** As described above.
2. **Select the Top Layer:** Tap on the layer that you want to merge *downwards*.
3. **Tap the Merge Icon:** Tap the merge icon (it looks like two overlapping squares merging into one) next to the trash can icon. The selected layer will be merged with the layer directly below it.

4. **Important Note:** Merging layers is a permanent action and cannot be undone with the undo function. If you need to revert the merge, you will have to manually undo your actions before merging.

VIII. Deleting a Layer (What to Press):

1. **Open the Layers Menu:** As described above.
2. **Select the Layer:** Tap on the layer you want to delete.
3. **Tap the Trash Can Icon:** Tap the trash can icon next to the layer's name.

IX. Use Cases for Layers:

- **Sketching and Drawing:** Use layers to separate different elements of your drawing, such as the background, foreground, and line art. This allows you to easily edit each element without affecting others.
- **Annotating PDFs:** Use a separate layer for your annotations so you can easily hide or show them without affecting the original PDF content.
- **Note-Taking with Diagrams:** Use one layer for your text notes and another layer for diagrams or sketches.
- **Iterative Design:** Use layers to explore different design options or variations without having to erase or redraw previous versions.
- **Tracing:** Import an image as the background layer and then use a separate layer to trace over it.

X. Tips and Tricks:

- **Name Your Layers:** While the reMarkable 2 doesn't offer direct renaming of layers, you can mentally associate each layer with a specific purpose (e.g., "Sketch," "Line Art," "Annotations").
- **Plan Your Layers:** Before you start working, think about how you want to organize your content using layers. This will save you time and effort later on.
- **Use Layer Visibility to Review Your Work:** Use the layer visibility feature to isolate different elements of your work and review them individually.
- **Be Mindful of the Layer Limit:** Remember that there is a limit to the number of layers you can use. Merge layers when appropriate to free up space.

CHAPTER 3

Advanced Note-Taking Techniques

Advanced Note-Taking Techniques builds upon the foundational skills covered in the previous chapter, exploring features that elevate your note-taking to a new level of efficiency and organization. This chapter delves into converting your handwritten notes into typed text, making them easily searchable and shareable. We'll also cover powerful organization tools like folders and tags, enabling you to manage a large library of notes effectively. Furthermore, you'll learn how to create links and hyperlinks within your notes, connecting related ideas and resources. We'll also explore creating tables and lists directly on your reMarkable, improving the structure and readability of your notes. Finally, we'll cover the essential skill of annotating PDFs and ebooks, turning your reMarkable 2 into a powerful document review and analysis tool. By the end of this chapter, you'll be equipped with advanced techniques to maximize the reMarkable 2's potential for productivity and knowledge management.

• *Converting handwriting to text*

The handwriting conversion feature on the reMarkable 2 allows you to transform your handwritten notes into typed text, making them searchable, editable on other devices, and easily shareable. This guide provides a detailed explanation of how to use this feature effectively, along with tips for optimizing its accuracy.

I. Enabling Handwriting Conversion:

Handwriting conversion must be enabled in the settings before you can use it.

1. **Access the Settings Menu (What to Press):**

   ○ Swipe down from the top of the screen to open the Quick Settings menu.
   ○ Tap the gear icon (Settings) in the top right corner.
2. **Navigate to Handwriting Conversion Settings (What to Press):**

   ○ In the Settings menu, tap on "Handwriting conversion".
3. **Enable Conversion (What to Press):**

   ○ Toggle the switch to enable handwriting conversion.
4. **Select Language:**

    ○ You can select the language that the remarkable will use when converting your handwriting to text. This is important as different languages have different characters and handwriting styles.

    ○

II. Converting Handwriting to Text:

There are two main ways to convert handwriting to text on the reMarkable 2: converting individual selections or converting entire pages.

A. Converting a Selection of Handwriting (What to Press):

This method is useful for converting specific parts of your notes.

1. **Select the Selection Tool (Lasso):** Tap the lasso icon in the toolbar.
2. **Select the Handwriting:** Draw a loop around the handwriting you want to convert. Ensure that all the characters you want to convert are fully enclosed within the lasso.

3. **Access Conversion Options (What to Press):** With the handwriting selected, tap the three vertical dots icon (More options) in the toolbar.

4. **Select "Convert to text" (What to Press):** Tap "Convert to text" from the menu.
5. **Review and Edit the Converted Text:** The converted text will appear in a text box. Review the text for any errors.

    ○ **Editing the Text (What to Press):** Tap inside the text box to activate the on-screen keyboard. Use the keyboard to correct any mistakes.

    ○
6. **Inserting the Converted Text (What to Press):** Once you are satisfied with the converted text, tap outside the text box. The text will be inserted into your notes.

B. Converting an Entire Page (What to Press):

This method is useful for converting all handwriting on a page at once.

1. **Access More Options:** Tap the three vertical dots icon (More options) in the toolbar.

2. **Select "Convert to text" (What to Press):** Tap "Convert to text" from the menu.

3. **Review and Edit the Converted Text:** The converted text will appear in a pop-up window. Review the text and edit any errors using the on-screen keyboard.

4. **Inserting the Converted Text (What to Press):** Tap the "Insert" button to insert the converted text onto the page as a text box.

III. Factors Affecting Conversion Accuracy:

Several factors can affect the accuracy of handwriting conversion:

- **Handwriting Style:** Clear, consistent handwriting with well-formed characters generally yields the best results. Cursive or very stylized handwriting can be more challenging for the conversion engine.
- **Spacing Between Characters and Words:** Adequate spacing between characters and words is crucial for accurate conversion. Avoid writing characters too close together or overlapping them.
- **Language:** Ensure that the correct language is selected in the handwriting conversion settings. The conversion engine is optimized for specific languages.
- **Note Quality:** Very light or faint handwriting may be difficult for the conversion engine to recognize.

IV. Tips for Improving Conversion Accuracy:

- **Write Clearly and Consistently:** Focus on forming your characters clearly and maintaining consistent spacing between them.
- **Write on the Lines (If Using Lined Templates):** Writing on the lines of a lined template can help improve the consistency of your handwriting and improve conversion accuracy.
- **Use the Zoom Function:** Zooming in can help you write more precisely, especially when writing small characters.
- **Practice:** The more you use the handwriting conversion feature, the better you'll become at writing in a way that the engine can understand.
- **Edit After Conversion:** Always review the converted text for errors and correct them using the on-screen keyboard.

V. Limitations:

- **No Real-Time Conversion:** The reMarkable 2 does not offer real-time handwriting conversion. You must manually initiate the conversion process.
- **Accuracy Varies:** The accuracy of the conversion depends on the factors mentioned above. It's not always perfect, and some manual editing may be required.
- **Formatting Loss:** Basic formatting like bolding, italics, or underlining is not preserved during conversion.

VI. Use Cases for Handwriting Conversion:

- **Creating Searchable Notes:** Converting your handwritten notes to text makes them searchable within the reMarkable 2 and on other devices via the reMarkable apps.
- **Sharing Notes Digitally:** Converted text can be easily copied and pasted into emails, documents, or other applications.
- **Editing Notes on Other Devices:** You can access and edit your converted notes on your computer or smartphone using the reMarkable apps.
- **Archiving Notes:** Converting your handwritten notes to text creates a digital record that can be easily stored and backed up.

By following these guidelines and tips, you can effectively use the handwriting conversion feature on the reMarkable 2 to transform your handwritten notes into useful digital text. While it may require some practice and occasional editing, this feature significantly enhances the versatility and utility of the device for note-taking and knowledge management.

Searching your notes

The ability to search your notes is a crucial feature for managing and retrieving information effectively. The reMarkable 2 offers powerful search capabilities that allow you to quickly locate specific keywords, phrases, or even handwritten content within your notebooks and documents.

I. Types of Searches:

The reMarkable 2 supports two main types of searches:

- **Text Search (Converted Handwriting):** This search type allows you to find typed text within your notes. This includes text that you have converted from handwriting using the handwriting conversion feature.
- **Handwriting Search (Beta/Experimental Feature):** This feature, which may be in beta or experimental phase depending on your reMarkable's software

version, attempts to find handwritten words directly, even if they haven't been converted to text. Its accuracy can vary depending on handwriting clarity.

II. Accessing the Search Function (What to Press):

The search function is accessible from the "My Files" screen and within open notebooks or documents.

A. From the "My Files" Screen:

1. **Tap the Magnifying Glass Icon:** Locate the magnifying glass icon in the top bar of the "My Files" screen.
2. **Tap the Icon:** Use your Marker to tap the magnifying glass icon. This will open the search bar.

B. From Within a Notebook or Document:

1. **Tap the Three Vertical Dots Icon (More Options):** Tap the three vertical dots icon in the top right corner of the screen.
2. **Select "Search" (What to Press):** From the menu that appears, tap "Search". This will open the search bar.

III. Performing a Text Search (Converted Handwriting):

This is the most reliable search method, as it searches through typed text.

1. **Open the Search Bar:** As described above.
2. **Enter Your Search Term (What to Press):** Use the on-screen keyboard to type the keyword or phrase you are looking for.
3. **Start the Search (What to Press):** Tap the "Enter" or "Search" key on the on-screen keyboard.

IV. Performing a Handwriting Search (Beta/Experimental Feature):

This feature is designed to search directly through your handwritten notes.

1. **Open the Search Bar:** As described above.
2. **Enter Your Search Term (What to Press):** Use the on-screen keyboard to type the keyword or phrase you are looking for.
3. **Start the Search (What to Press):** Tap the "Enter" or "Search" key on the on-screen keyboard.

V. Understanding Search Results:

The search results are displayed as a list of pages where the search term was found.

- **Preview:** Each search result shows a small preview of the page where the search term was found, with the search term highlighted.
- **Navigating to the Result (What to Press):** Tap on a search result to open the corresponding page in your notebook or document.

VI. Refining Your Search:

- **Exact Phrase Search:** To search for an exact phrase, enclose the phrase in quotation marks (e.g., "meeting minutes").
- **Case Sensitivity:** Searches are generally not case-sensitive. Searching for "Meeting" will find both "meeting" and "Meeting."
- **Partial Word Search:** You can search for partial words. For example, searching for "meet" will find "meeting," "meets," and "meetup."

VII. Factors Affecting Search Accuracy:

- **Handwriting Clarity (Handwriting Search):** The accuracy of handwriting search depends heavily on the clarity and consistency of your handwriting. Clear, well-formed characters are more likely to be recognized correctly.
- **Handwriting Conversion Accuracy (Text Search):** If you are searching for converted handwriting, the accuracy of the search depends on the accuracy of the initial handwriting conversion.
- **Note Quality:** Very light or faint handwriting may be difficult for the search engine to recognize, especially in handwriting search.

VIII. Tips for Optimizing Search Results:

- **Convert Handwriting to Text Whenever Possible:** Converting your handwriting to text ensures the most accurate and reliable search results.
- **Use Clear and Consistent Handwriting:** If you rely on the handwriting search feature, practice writing clearly and consistently.
- **Use Descriptive Titles and Headings:** Using descriptive titles and headings in your notebooks can improve search accuracy and make it easier to find relevant information.
- **Organize Your Notes with Folders and Tags:** Organizing your notes into folders and using tags can help you narrow down your search and find information more quickly.

IX. Limitations:

- **Handwriting Search Accuracy:** The handwriting search feature is still under development, and its accuracy can vary. It's best used as a supplementary search method alongside text search.
- **No Search Within PDFs (Without Conversion):** You cannot directly search for handwritten or typed text *within* imported PDFs unless you have converted the PDF to a reMarkable notebook page (which is not a true conversion, but creates a rasterized image that can be annotated). Annotation search *within* the annotation layer is possible.
- **No Search Within Ebooks:** Similar to PDFs, you cannot search within ebooks.

X. Use Cases for Searching Your Notes:

- **Finding Specific Information:** Quickly locate key facts, figures, or ideas within your notes.
- **Reviewing Meeting Minutes:** Search for specific action items or decisions made during meetings.
- **Locating Research Notes:** Find relevant information from your research notes for writing papers or reports.
- **Retrieving Ideas from Brainstorming Sessions:** Quickly access specific ideas or concepts from your brainstorming notes.

By understanding how to use the search function effectively, you can unlock the true power of your reMarkable 2 as a digital notebook and information management tool. Whether you're searching for converted text or relying on the handwriting search feature, the reMarkable 2 offers powerful tools to help you find the information you need quickly and efficiently.

• *Organizing notebooks with folders and tags*

The ability to search your notes is a crucial feature for managing and retrieving information effectively. The reMarkable 2 offers powerful search capabilities that allow you to quickly locate specific keywords, phrases, or even handwritten content within your notebooks and documents. This guide provides a comprehensive overview of how to use the search function, along with tips for optimizing your search results.

I. Types of Searches:

The reMarkable 2 supports two main types of searches:

- **Text Search (Converted Handwriting):** This search type allows you to find typed text within your notes. This includes text that you have converted from handwriting using the handwriting conversion feature.
- **Handwriting Search (Beta/Experimental Feature):** This feature, which may be in beta or experimental phase depending on your reMarkable's software version, attempts to find handwritten words directly, even if they haven't been converted to text. Its accuracy can vary depending on handwriting clarity.

II. Accessing the Search Function (What to Press):

The search function is accessible from the "My Files" screen and within open notebooks or documents.

A. From the "My Files" Screen:

1. **Tap the Magnifying Glass Icon:** Locate the magnifying glass icon in the top bar of the "My Files" screen.
2. **Tap the Icon:** Use your Marker to tap the magnifying glass icon. This will open the search bar.

B. From Within a Notebook or Document:

1. **Tap the Three Vertical Dots Icon (More Options):** Tap the three vertical dots icon in the top right corner of the screen.
2. **Select "Search" (What to Press):** From the menu that appears, tap "Search". This will open the search bar.

III. Performing a Text Search (Converted Handwriting):

This is the most reliable search method, as it searches through typed text.

1. **Open the Search Bar:** As described above.
2. **Enter Your Search Term (What to Press):** Use the on-screen keyboard to type the keyword or phrase you are looking for.
3. **Start the Search (What to Press):** Tap the "Enter" or "Search" key on the on-screen keyboard.

IV. Performing a Handwriting Search (Beta/Experimental Feature):

This feature is designed to search directly through your handwritten notes.

1. **Open the Search Bar:** As described above.
2. **Enter Your Search Term (What to Press):** Use the on-screen keyboard to type the keyword or phrase you are looking for.

3. **Start the Search (What to Press):** Tap the "Enter" or "Search" key on the on-screen keyboard.

V. Understanding Search Results:

The search results are displayed as a list of pages where the search term was found.

- **Preview:** Each search result shows a small preview of the page where the search term was found, with the search term highlighted.
-
- **Navigating to the Result (What to Press):** Tap on a search result to open the corresponding page in your notebook or document.

VI. Refining Your Search:

- **Exact Phrase Search:** To search for an exact phrase, enclose the phrase in quotation marks (e.g., "meeting minutes").
- **Case Sensitivity:** Searches are generally not case-sensitive. Searching for "Meeting" will find both "meeting" and "Meeting."
- **Partial Word Search:** You can search for partial words. For example, searching for "meet" will find "meeting," "meets," and "meetup."

VII. Factors Affecting Search Accuracy:

- **Handwriting Clarity (Handwriting Search):** The accuracy of handwriting search depends heavily on the clarity and consistency of your handwriting. Clear, well-formed characters are more likely to be recognized correctly.
- **Handwriting Conversion Accuracy (Text Search):** If you are searching for converted handwriting, the accuracy of the search depends on the accuracy of the initial handwriting conversion.
- **Note Quality:** Very light or faint handwriting may be difficult for the search engine to recognize, especially in handwriting search.

VIII. Tips for Optimizing Search Results:

- **Convert Handwriting to Text Whenever Possible:** Converting your handwriting to text ensures the most accurate and reliable search results.
- **Use Clear and Consistent Handwriting:** If you rely on the handwriting search feature, practice writing clearly and consistently.
- **Use Descriptive Titles and Headings:** Using descriptive titles and headings in your notebooks can improve search accuracy and make it easier to find relevant information.

- **Organize Your Notes with Folders and Tags:** Organizing your notes into folders and using tags can help you narrow down your search and find information more quickly.
-

IX. Limitations:

- **Handwriting Search Accuracy:** The handwriting search feature is still under development, and its accuracy can vary. It's best used as a supplementary search method alongside text search.
- **No Search Within PDFs (Without Conversion):** You cannot directly search for handwritten or typed text *within* imported PDFs unless you have converted the PDF to a reMarkable notebook page (which is not a true conversion, but creates a rasterized image that can be annotated). Annotation search *within* the annotation layer is possible.
- **No Search Within Ebooks:** Similar to PDFs, you cannot search within ebooks.

X. Use Cases for Searching Your Notes:

- **Finding Specific Information:** Quickly locate key facts, figures, or ideas within your notes.
- **Reviewing Meeting Minutes:** Search for specific action items or decisions made during meetings.
- **Locating Research Notes:** Find relevant information from your research notes for writing papers or reports.
- **Retrieving Ideas from Brainstorming Sessions:** Quickly access specific ideas or concepts from your brainstorming notes.

By understanding how to use the search function effectively, you can unlock the true power of your reMarkable 2 as a digital notebook and information management tool. Whether you're searching for converted text or relying on the handwriting search feature, the reMarkable 2 offers powerful tools to help you find the information you need quickly and efficiently.

Organizing Notebooks with Folders and Tags on the reMarkable 2

As your library of notes grows on your reMarkable 2, effective organization becomes crucial for quickly finding and managing your content. Folders and tags are the primary tools for organizing your notebooks and documents, providing different ways to categorize and filter your information. This guide explains how to use folders and tags effectively to keep your reMarkable 2 organized.

I. Using Folders:

Folders provide a hierarchical structure for organizing your notebooks and documents, similar to folders on a computer.

A. Creating a New Folder (What to Press):

1. **Go to the "My Files" Screen:** Ensure you are on the main "My Files" screen.
2. **Tap the "+" Button:** Tap the "+" button in the top bar.
3. **Select "New folder" (What to Press):** From the menu that appears, tap "New folder".
4. **Name the Folder (What to Press):** Use the on-screen keyboard to type a name for the folder.
5. **Confirm the Name (What to Press):** Tap the checkmark or "Done" button on the keyboard.

B. Moving Notebooks and Documents into Folders (What to Press):

1. **Select the Item(s):** Tap and hold on the notebook or document you want to move until a checkmark appears. You can select multiple items by tapping on other items.
2. **Access the More Options Menu (What to Press):** Tap the three vertical dots icon (More options) in the top bar.
3. **Select "Move" (What to Press):** Tap "Move" from the menu.
4. **Choose the Destination Folder (What to Press):** Navigate to the folder where you want to move the item(s) and tap on it.
5. **Confirm the Move (What to Press):** Tap "Move here".

C. Creating Subfolders:

You can create folders within folders (subfolders) to create a more granular organization. The process is the same as creating a new folder, but you do it while inside another folder.

1. **Open the Parent Folder:** Tap on the folder where you want to create a subfolder.
2. **Create a New Folder:** Follow the steps for creating a new folder (as described above).

D. Renaming a Folder (What to Press):

1. **Select the Folder:** Tap and hold on the folder you want to rename.
2. **Access the More Options Menu (What to Press):** Tap the three vertical dots icon (More options) that appears.
3. **Select "Rename" (What to Press):** Tap "Rename".
4. **Enter the New Name (What to Press):** Use the on-screen keyboard to type the new name.
5. **Confirm the Name (What to Press):** Tap the checkmark or "Done" button on the keyboard.

E. Deleting a Folder (What to Press):

1. **Select the Folder:** Tap and hold on the folder you want to delete.
2. **Tap the Trash Can Icon:** Tap the trash can icon that appears in the top bar.
3. **Confirm Deletion:** Confirm that you want to delete the folder. Note that deleting a folder will also delete all the contents within it.

II. Using Tags:

Tags provide a more flexible way to categorize your notes, allowing you to associate multiple categories with a single notebook or document.

A. Adding a Tag (What to Press):

1. **Select the Item(s):** Tap and hold on the notebook or document to which you want to add a tag. You can select multiple items.
2. **Access the More Options Menu (What to Press):** Tap the three vertical dots icon (More options) in the top bar.
3. **Select "Add tags" (What to Press):** Tap "Add tags".
4. **Type the Tag Name (What to Press):** Use the on-screen keyboard to type the tag name.
5. **Confirm the Tag (What to Press):** Tap the "+" button or the "Enter" key on the keyboard to create and add the tag.

B. Viewing Items with a Specific Tag (What to Press):

1. **Tap the Three Horizontal Lines Icon (Filter):** In the "My Files" view, tap the icon that looks like three horizontal lines (the filter icon) in the top bar.
2. **Select the Tag:** Tap on the tag you want to filter by. Only notebooks and documents with that tag will be displayed.
3. **Clear the Filter (What to Press):** To view all your files again, tap the "x" next to the selected tag in the filter menu.

C. Removing a Tag (What to Press):

1. **Select the Item(s):** Tap and hold on the notebook or document from which you want to remove a tag.
2. **Access the More Options Menu (What to Press):** Tap the three vertical dots icon (More options).
3. **Select "Edit tags" (What to Press):** Tap "Edit tags".
4. **Tap the "x" next to the Tag:** Tap the "x" next to the tag you want to remove.

III. Best Practices for Organizing with Folders and Tags:

- **Plan Your Folder Structure:** Before creating a large number of folders, take some time to plan a logical structure that will work for you. Consider broad categories and then create subfolders within them.
- **Use Tags for Cross-Referencing:** Use tags to connect related notebooks and documents that might be located in different folders.
- **Be Consistent with Tagging:** Use consistent tag names and avoid creating too many similar tags.
- **Combine Folders and Tags:** Folders and tags work best in combination. Use folders for broad organization and tags for more specific categorization and cross-referencing.
- **Regularly Review and Organize:** Periodically review your folder structure and tags to ensure they are still effective and make any necessary adjustments.
- **Examples:**
  - **Folders:** "Work," "Personal," "Projects," "Courses"
  - **Tags:** "Meeting Notes," "Project X," "Research," "To Do," "Important"

By effectively using folders and tags, you can create a well-organized and easily navigable library of notes on your reMarkable 2. This will save you time and effort when searching for information and improve your overall productivity.

• *Creating tables and lists*

I. Creating Tables:

Since there's no automatic table insertion, you'll be drawing the table structure yourself. Here's how:

1. **Choose Your Tool:** The Fineliner pen tool is generally best for creating clean, straight lines for tables.

2. **Draw the Outline:** Start by drawing the outer rectangle of your table. Use the shape recognition feature (draw a rough rectangle and hold your pen at the end)

to create a perfect rectangle.

3. **Draw the Rows and Columns:** Use the Fineliner to draw horizontal lines for the rows and vertical lines for the columns. Again, use the line straightening feature (draw a rough line and hold) to ensure straight lines.

4. **Adjust and Refine:** If your lines aren't perfectly aligned, you can use the eraser to make corrections or the selection tool (lasso) to move and resize lines.

Tips for Tables:

- **Plan Ahead:** Before you start drawing, sketch out a rough layout of your table to determine the number of rows and columns you need.
- **Use a Grid Template:** Using a grid template as the background for your notebook can help you draw straight lines and create evenly spaced rows and columns.
- **Use the Zoom Function:** Zooming in can help you draw more precise lines, especially for smaller tables.
- **Consider Layers:** If you anticipate needing to make changes to your table structure later, consider drawing the table on a separate layer. This will allow you to edit the table without affecting your notes.

II. Creating Lists:

There are a few ways to create lists on the Remarkable 2, each with its own advantages:

A. Simple Bulleted or Numbered Lists (Manual):

1. **Choose Your Tool:** Use the pen, marker, or pencil tool, depending on your preference.
2. **Draw Bullets or Numbers:** Manually draw bullet points (small circles or dots) or write numbers at the beginning of each list item.
3. **Write Your List Items:** Write your list items next to the bullets or numbers.

B. Using the Checklists Template:

The Remarkable 2 offers a "Checklists" template that provides pre-made checkboxes.

1. **Create a New Notebook or Change Template:** When creating a new notebook, select the "Checklists" template. Or, in an existing notebook, go to the More Options menu and select "Change template" to switch to the "Checklists" template.

2. **Write Your List Items:** Write your list items next to the checkboxes.
3. **Check Off Items:** You can tap the checkboxes with your pen to mark items as complete.

C. Creating Lists with the Shape Tool (Lines):

You can use the line straightening feature to create consistent vertical lines for a more structured list.

1. **Choose the Fineliner Tool.**
2. **Draw a Vertical Line:** Draw a short vertical line and hold your pen to straighten it. This will serve as a visual separator for your list items.
3. **Write Your List Items:** Write your list items next to the vertical lines.

Tips for Lists:

- **Spacing:** Pay attention to the spacing between list items to ensure readability.
- **Consistency:** Try to maintain consistent bullet or number styles throughout your list.
- **Combine with Other Tools:** You can use the highlighter to emphasize important list items or the selection tool to move list items around.

III. Limitations:

- **No Automatic Table/List Formatting:** The Remarkable 2 does not automatically format tables or lists like dedicated word processing software. You have to create the structure manually.
- **No Table Formulas or Sorting:** You cannot perform calculations or sort data within tables on the Remarkable 2.
- **Limited List Styles:** You are limited to manually drawn bullets or numbers or the pre-made checkboxes in the "Checklists" template.

IV. Workarounds and Alternatives:

- **Create Tables/Lists in Another Application:** For complex tables or lists with advanced formatting or calculations, it's often best to create them in a word processor or spreadsheet application and then import them as PDFs to your Remarkable 2.
- **Use Templates:** Explore online resources for Remarkable templates. Some users create and share custom templates that include pre-made table or list structures.

V. Use Cases:

- **Tables:** Creating simple data tables, comparison charts, or schedules.
- **Lists:** Making to-do lists, grocery lists, outlines, or brainstorming ideas.

While the Remarkable 2 doesn't offer dedicated table and list tools, the methods described above provide effective workarounds for creating structured content within your notes. By using these techniques and tips, you can enhance the organization and readability of your digital notebooks.

Annotating PDFs and ebooks

The reMarkable 2 shines as a device for annotating PDFs and ebooks, offering a natural, paper-like experience for marking up documents, adding comments, and highlighting key information. This guide provides a comprehensive overview of how to annotate PDFs and ebooks on your reMarkable 2.

I. Importing PDFs and Ebooks:

Before you can annotate a PDF or ebook, you need to import it onto your reMarkable 2.

1. **Using the reMarkable Desktop App:** The easiest way to import files is using the reMarkable desktop application.

   - **Open the reMarkable Desktop App:** Launch the app on your computer.
   - **Drag and Drop or Use the Import Function:** Drag and drop the PDF or ebook file into the app window, or click the import button and select the file from your computer.
   - **Sync:** The file will automatically sync to your reMarkable 2.
2. **Using the reMarkable Mobile App:** You can also import files using the mobile app, though this is less common for large PDF files.

   - **Open the reMarkable Mobile App:** Launch the app on your phone or tablet.
   - **Use the Import Function:** Look for an import or "+" button, and select the PDF or ebook from your device's storage or a cloud service.
   - **Sync:** The file will sync to your reMarkable 2.
3. **Directly from USB (Less Common):** You can connect your reMarkable 2 to your computer via USB and transfer files directly. This is generally less convenient than using the apps.

Supported File Formats:

- **PDF:** The reMarkable 2 primarily supports PDF files for annotation.
- **EPUB:** The reMarkable 2 supports EPUB files for ebook reading, but annotation features may be limited compared to PDFs.

II. Annotating PDFs:

Once you've imported a PDF, you can begin annotating it.

1. **Open the PDF:** Tap on the PDF file in the "My Files" view to open it.

2. **Using the Toolbar:** The toolbar at the top of the screen provides the tools you'll use for annotation.

   - **Pen, Marker, and Pencil:** Use these tools to write, draw, highlight, underline, or add freehand annotations directly on the PDF.
   - **Eraser:** Use the eraser to remove your annotations.
   - **Selection Tool (Lasso):** Use the selection tool to select and move or delete annotations.
   - **Zoom:** Use the zoom function to zoom in for more precise annotations.
3. **Adding Comments:** You can add written comments directly to the PDF using the pen, marker, or pencil tool.

III. Annotating Ebooks (EPUB):

Annotation features for EPUB ebooks are generally more limited than for PDFs.

1. **Open the EPUB:** Tap on the EPUB file in the "My Files" view to open it.

2. **Basic Annotations:** You can usually use the pen, marker, and eraser tools to make basic annotations, such as highlighting or underlining text.

3. **Limited Functionality:** Features like adding comments or more advanced markup tools may not be available for EPUB files.

IV. Key Considerations for Annotating:

- **Non-Destructive Annotations:** Your annotations are saved as a separate layer on top of the original PDF or ebook file. This means that the original file remains unchanged.
- **Syncing Annotations:** Your annotations are synced to the reMarkable cloud, allowing you to access them from other devices using the reMarkable apps.

- **Exporting Annotations:** You can export the annotated PDF as a new PDF file, which will include your annotations. This allows you to share your annotated documents with others who don't have a reMarkable.

V. Tips and Tricks for Effective Annotation:

- **Use Different Colors for Different Purposes:** Use different colors for different types of annotations, such as highlighting key passages, adding comments, or marking questions.
- **Use Layers for Complex Annotations:** If you're making complex annotations, consider using layers to organize different elements.
- **Zoom In for Precision:** Zoom in for more precise annotations, especially when working with small text or detailed diagrams.
- **Use the Selection Tool for Editing:** Use the selection tool to move, resize, or delete annotations.
- **Combine Annotations with Other Features:** Combine annotations with other reMarkable features, such as handwriting conversion or searching, to enhance your workflow.

VI. Limitations:

- **No Direct Text Editing in PDFs:** You cannot directly edit the text within a PDF on the reMarkable 2. You can only annotate it.
- **Limited EPUB Annotation Features:** As mentioned earlier, annotation features for EPUB files are more limited than for PDFs.
- **Large PDF Performance:** Very large or complex PDFs may experience performance issues, such as slow loading times or laggy annotation.

VII. Use Cases for Annotating PDFs and Ebooks:

- **Reviewing Documents:** Marking up reports, contracts, or other documents.
- **Reading and Studying:** Highlighting key passages, adding notes, and summarizing information in textbooks or research papers.
- **Proofreading:** Marking up drafts of written work.
- **Giving Feedback:** Providing feedback on design mockups, presentations, or other visual materials.

By using the reMarkable 2 for annotating PDFs and ebooks, you can combine the benefits of digital technology with the natural feel of pen and paper, creating a powerful and efficient workflow for document review and analysis.

CHAPTER 4

<u>Working with Documents</u>

Working with Documents focuses on how the reMarkable 2 interacts with external files, transforming it from a standalone note-taking device into a versatile document management tool. This chapter covers importing PDFs and ebooks, turning your reMarkable 2 into a powerful document review and reading platform. We'll explore the annotation and markup capabilities in detail, showing you how to effectively interact with these imported files. Furthermore, you'll learn how to export your work in various formats (PDF, PNG, SVG) for sharing or further editing on other platforms. This chapter also details the functionality of the reMarkable desktop app, which streamlines file transfer and management. Finally, we'll discuss the integration with cloud services like Google Drive and Dropbox, enabling seamless synchronization and access to your files across multiple devices. By the end of this chapter, you'll be able to efficiently manage, annotate, and share your documents using the reMarkable 2.

• *Importing PDFs and ebooks*

Importing PDFs and ebooks is a core function of the reMarkable 2, transforming it into a powerful tool for document review, reading, and annotation. This guide provides a detailed walkthrough of the various methods for importing files, along with important considerations and troubleshooting tips.

I. Supported File Formats:

The reMarkable 2 primarily supports the following file formats:

- **PDF (.pdf):** This is the most widely supported format and the one for which the reMarkable 2 offers the richest annotation features.
- **EPUB (.epub):** This is a common ebook format. While the reMarkable 2 can display EPUB files, annotation functionality is typically more limited compared to PDFs.
-

II. Importing Methods:

There are three primary methods for importing files to your reMarkable 2: using the desktop app, using the mobile app, and using a USB connection. The desktop app is generally the most efficient and recommended method, especially for larger files.

A. Using the reMarkable Desktop App (Recommended):

The reMarkable desktop app provides a seamless and convenient way to transfer files.

1. **Install the Desktop App:** Download and install the reMarkable desktop app from the official reMarkable website ([invalid URL removed]).
2. **Open the Desktop App:** Launch the app on your computer.

3. **Sign In:** Sign in to the app using your reMarkable account credentials (the same email address and password you use on your reMarkable 2).

4. **Importing Files (What to Press/Click):** There are two ways to import files using the desktop app:

   - **Drag and Drop:** The simplest method is to drag and drop the PDF or EPUB file directly into the app window.
   -
   - **Using the Import Button (What to Click):** Alternatively, you can click the "Import" button (it may be represented by a "+" icon or the word "Import") within the app. This will open a file browser window where you can select the file you want to import.
5. **Synchronization:** Once you've added a file to the desktop app, it will automatically begin synchronizing with your reMarkable 2 via the reMarkable cloud. Make sure both your computer and reMarkable 2 are connected to the internet for synchronization to occur.

6. **Viewing Imported Files on Your reMarkable 2:** The imported file will appear in the "My Files" view on your reMarkable 2, usually within a few seconds or minutes, depending on the file size and your internet connection.

B. Using the reMarkable Mobile App:

The mobile app also allows you to import files, though it's generally better suited for smaller files due to potential limitations with mobile data and storage.

1. **Install the Mobile App:** Download and install the reMarkable mobile app from your device's app store (iOS App Store or Google Play Store).
2. **Open the Mobile App:** Launch the app on your smartphone or tablet.

3. **Sign In:** Sign in to the app using your reMarkable account credentials.

4. **Importing Files (What to Press/Tap):** The exact steps may vary slightly depending on the app version and your mobile operating system, but generally, you'll find an import or "+" button.

   - **Locate the Import Option:** Look for a "+" icon, an "Import" button, or an option to add a file from your device.
   - **Select the File (What to Tap):** Tap the import option. This will open your device's file browser, allowing you to select the PDF or EPUB file you want to import. You might be able to import from local storage, cloud storage (like Google Drive or iCloud), or other apps that share files.
   -

5. **Synchronization:** Similar to the desktop app, the imported file will synchronize with your reMarkable 2 via the reMarkable cloud.
6. **Viewing Imported Files on Your reMarkable 2:** The imported file will appear in the "My Files" view on your reMarkable 2.

C. Using a USB Connection (Less Recommended):

While possible, importing via USB is generally less convenient than using the apps.

1. **Connect Your reMarkable 2 to Your Computer:** Use the USB-C cable that came with your reMarkable 2 to connect it to a USB port on your computer.
2. **reMarkable as a Mass Storage Device:** Your reMarkable 2 will typically appear as a mass storage device (like a USB flash drive) on your computer.

3. **Locate the "documents" Folder:** Open the reMarkable 2's storage on your computer and navigate to the "documents" folder.

4. **Copy Files:** Copy the PDF or EPUB files you want to import into the "documents" folder.

5. **Disconnect Your reMarkable 2:** Safely eject or disconnect your reMarkable 2 from your computer.

6. **Viewing Imported Files on Your reMarkable 2:** The imported files will appear in the "My Files" view on your reMarkable 2.

III. Important Considerations for Importing:

- **File Size:** Very large PDF files (especially those with many images or complex graphics) may take longer to import and may affect the reMarkable 2's performance.
- **PDF Complexity:** Highly complex PDFs with intricate layouts or unusual formatting may not display perfectly on the reMarkable 2.
- **DRM-Protected Ebooks:** Ebooks with digital rights management (DRM) protection may not be compatible with the reMarkable 2.
-
- **File Organization:** The reMarkable 2 preserves the folder structure of files you import. So if you have your PDFs organized into folders on your computer, that folder structure will be reflected on your reMarkable 2 after syncing.

IV. Troubleshooting Import Issues:

- **Files Not Syncing:** Ensure that both your computer/mobile device and your reMarkable 2 are connected to the internet and that you are signed in to the same reMarkable account on all devices. Try restarting your reMarkable 2 or the reMarkable app.
- **File Format Not Supported:** Double-check that the file you are trying to import is a PDF or EPUB. Other file formats are not directly supported.
- **File Corruption:** If a file is corrupted, it may not import correctly. Try downloading the file again from its original source.
- **Storage Space:** Ensure that you have enough free storage space on your reMarkable 2.

V. Best Practices for Importing:

- **Use the Desktop App for Large Files:** For large PDFs or multiple files, the desktop app is the most efficient import method.
- **Organize Your Files Before Importing:** Organize your files into folders on your computer before importing them to maintain a good structure on your reMarkable 2.
- **Check PDF Compatibility:** If you encounter display issues with a PDF, try using a PDF optimization tool on your computer before importing it. This can sometimes reduce file size and improve compatibility.

- *Annotating and marking up documents*

The reMarkable 2 truly shines when it comes to annotating and marking up documents, providing a digital paper experience that closely mimics traditional pen-on-paper workflows. This guide will delve into the various annotation tools and techniques, empowering you to effectively interact with your PDFs and ebooks.

I. Opening a PDF or Ebook:

1. **Locate the File:** Navigate to the "My Files" view on your reMarkable 2.
2. **Tap to Open:** Tap on the PDF or ebook file you want to annotate. The document will open, displaying the first page.

II. The Annotation Toolbar:

Once a document is open, the toolbar at the top of the screen provides access to the annotation tools.

- **1. Pen Tool (What to Press):**

  - **Icon:** A pen nib.
  - **Function:** Use this for writing notes, adding comments, drawing diagrams, or making freehand markings.
  - **Options (Tap again):** Tapping the pen icon again allows you to choose different pen types (ballpoint, fineliner, marker, calligraphy), adjust thickness, and select a color (black, gray, white, and sometimes more).

- **2. Marker Tool (What to Press):**

  - **Icon:** A marker tip.
  - **Function:** Use this for highlighting text or creating broad strokes.
  - **Options (Tap again):** Tapping the marker icon again allows you to adjust thickness and color.

- **3. Pencil Tool (What to Press):**

  - **Icon:** A pencil tip.
  - **Function:** Simulates a graphite pencil, with shading effects based on pressure.
  - **Options (Tap again):** Adjust the thickness of the pencil "lead."

- **4. Eraser Tool (What to Press):**

  - **Icon:** An eraser.
  - **Function:** Erases your annotations.
  - **Options (Tap again):** Choose between the standard eraser (erases by rubbing) and the stroke eraser (erases entire strokes with a single tap).

- **5. Selection Tool (Lasso) (What to Press):**

- ○ **Icon:** A lasso.
- ○ **Function:** Selects annotations for moving, resizing, copying, cutting, or deleting.
- ○ **How to Use:** Draw a loop around the annotations you want to select.
- **6. Undo/Redo Arrows (What to Press):**

  - ○ **Icons:** Curved arrows pointing left (undo) and right (redo).
  - ○ **Function:** Undo reverses your last action; redo reapplies an undone action.
- **7. Zoom (What to Press):**

  - ○ **Icon:** A magnifying glass.
  - ○ **Function:** Zooms in or out of the document for more detailed work or a broader view. You can also use pinch-to-zoom gestures.
- **8. Page Overview (What to Press):**

  - ○ **Icon:** Four squares.
  - ○ **Function:** Opens a thumbnail view of all pages in the document, allowing you to quickly navigate to different pages.
- **9. More Options (Three Vertical Dots) (What to Press):**

  - ○ **Icon:** Three vertical dots.
  - ○ **Function:** This menu contains additional options:
    - ■ **Add page:** Inserts a blank page within the PDF for extra note-taking space.
    - ■ **Rotate:** Rotates the current page.
    - ■ **Adjust view:** Allows you to change how the PDF is displayed (e.g., fit to width, fit to page).

III. Annotation Techniques:

- **Highlighting:** Use the marker tool to highlight important text passages.
- **Underlining:** Use the pen or marker tool to underline key phrases or sentences.
- **Marginalia:** Use the pen or pencil tool to add notes, comments, or questions in the margins of the document.
- **Freehand Drawings and Diagrams:** Use the pen, marker, or pencil tool to create diagrams, sketches, or other visual annotations.
- **Adding Note Pages:** If you need more space for notes than the margins provide, use the "Add page" option in the More Options menu to insert blank pages within the PDF.

IV. Working with Layers (for Complex Annotations):

Using layers can be beneficial for more complex annotation tasks.

1. **Open the Layers Menu (What to Press):** Tap the stacked papers icon in the toolbar.

2. **Add a New Layer (What to Press):** Tap "Add Layer."

3. **Annotate on the New Layer:** Now, your annotations will be on a separate layer, allowing you to:

   - **Hide or Show Annotations:** Toggle the visibility of the annotation layer without affecting the original document.
   - **Move Annotations Independently:** Use the selection tool to move annotations without affecting the underlying text.
   - **Delete Annotations Without Affecting the Original:** Delete the entire annotation layer without altering the PDF.

V. Exporting Annotated PDFs:

Once you've finished annotating, you can export the PDF with your annotations included.

1. **Access the More Options Menu (What to Press):** Tap the three vertical dots icon in the toolbar.

2. **Select "Export PDF" (What to Press):** Tap "Export PDF".

3. **Choose Export Options (What to Press):** Select if you want to export the PDF with or without your annotations.

4. **Send the PDF:** The annotated PDF can be sent via email or saved to your reMarkable cloud storage for access on other devices.

VI. Annotating Ebooks (EPUBs):

Annotation functionality for EPUBs is more basic. You can typically use the pen, marker, and eraser tools to make simple markings, but features like adding separate note pages or using layers are generally not available.

VII. Key Advantages of Annotating on the reMarkable 2:

- **Paper-Like Experience:** The textured surface and low latency of the reMarkable 2 provide a writing experience that closely resembles pen on paper, making annotation feel natural and intuitive.
- **Focus and Distraction-Free Environment:** The lack of notifications and other distractions allows for focused reading and annotation.
- **Organization and Accessibility:** Your annotated documents are synced to the reMarkable cloud, making them accessible across your devices.

● *Exporting documents as PDF, PNG, or SVG*

Exporting your work from the reMarkable 2 allows you to share your notes, drawings, and annotated documents with others or preserve them in different file formats for use on other devices and platforms.

I. Exporting from a Notebook or PDF:

The export process is similar whether you are exporting a native reMarkable notebook or an annotated PDF.

1. **Open the Notebook or PDF:** Open the notebook or PDF you wish to export.

2. **Access the More Options Menu (What to Press):** Tap the three vertical dots icon (More options) in the toolbar.

3. **Select "Export PDF", "Export PNG" or "Export SVG" (What to Press):** From the menu that appears, choose the export format you want:

   - **Export PDF:** Exports the document as a PDF file. This is the most common format for sharing documents and preserving formatting. You'll have the option to export with or without your annotations.
   - **Export PNG:** Exports the current page as a PNG image file. This is useful for sharing individual pages as images.
   - **Export SVG:** Exports the current page as a vector graphic in SVG format. This is ideal for preserving the scalability of your drawings and diagrams, especially if you plan to edit them in vector graphics software.

4. **Choosing Export Options (If Applicable):**

   - **Export PDF with/without annotations:** If you selected "Export PDF", you will get a prompt to select if you wish to export the PDF with or without your annotations.

5. **Sending the Exported File (What to Press):** After selecting the export format, you'll be presented with sharing options. The options presented may vary depending on your reMarkable's software version. Common options include:

   - **Email:** Send the exported file directly via email. You will be prompted to enter recipient email addresses and optionally include a message.
   - **reMarkable Cloud/Cloud Storage:** The file can be saved to your reMarkable cloud storage which then syncs and allows you to access it from the desktop and mobile apps. This is the most convenient method for accessing the exported files on your computer or phone.
   - **USB (Less Common):** In some cases, you may be able to connect your reMarkable 2 to your computer via USB and directly access the exported files from its storage.

II. Understanding the Export Formats:

- **PDF (.pdf):**

  - **Preserves Layout:** Maintains the original layout and formatting of your document.
  - **Widely Compatible:** Can be opened on virtually any device with a PDF reader.
  - **Good for Printing:** Suitable for printing high-quality copies of your documents.
  - **Annotations Included (If Selected):** If you choose to export with annotations, your markings will be included in the PDF.

- **PNG (.png):**

  - **Image Format:** Exports the current page as a raster image.
  - **Lossless Compression:** Uses lossless compression, meaning no image data is lost during compression.
  - **Good for Sharing Images:** Suitable for sharing individual pages as images on social media or in presentations.
  - **Not Scalable:** Resizing a PNG image can result in pixelation.

- **SVG (.svg):**

  - **Vector Format:** Exports the current page as a vector graphic.
  - **Scalable:** Can be scaled to any size without loss of quality.
  - **Editable in Vector Graphics Software:** Can be opened and edited in vector graphics software like Adobe Illustrator or Inkscape.

- **Best for Drawings and Diagrams:** Ideal for exporting drawings, diagrams, and other vector-based content.

III. Exporting Multiple Pages (Indirectly):

The reMarkable 2 doesn't have a direct option to export multiple pages as separate files in one go. You will need to export each page individually.

Workaround for Multiple Pages:

- **Export as PDF:** The most effective way to "export multiple pages" is to export the entire notebook or PDF as a single PDF file. This will preserve all pages in one document.

IV. Exporting Annotated PDFs:

When exporting an annotated PDF, you have the option to include or exclude your annotations.

- **Exporting with Annotations:** This creates a new PDF file that includes your markings. This is useful for sharing your annotated document with others.
- **Exporting without Annotations:** This creates a clean copy of the original PDF without your markings. This is useful for preserving a clean version of the original document.

V. Troubleshooting Export Issues:

- **Export Fails:** If the export process fails, try restarting your reMarkable 2.
- **File Size Issues:** Very large notebooks or PDFs may take longer to export.
- **Formatting Issues (PDF):** While PDF export generally preserves formatting well, some complex layouts may not translate perfectly.

VI. Use Cases for Exporting:

- **Sharing Notes with Others:** Exporting as PDF allows you to share your notes with people who don't have a reMarkable 2.
- **Printing Your Work:** Exporting as PDF allows you to print high-quality copies of your notes or drawings.
- **Editing in Other Applications:** Exporting as SVG allows you to edit your drawings and diagrams in vector graphics software.
- **Backing Up Your Work:** Exporting your notebooks as PDFs provides an extra layer of backup in addition to cloud syncing.

By understanding the different export formats and options, you can effectively share and preserve your work created on the reMarkable 2. This flexibility makes the device a valuable tool for a variety of workflows.

● *Using the reMarkable desktop app*

The reMarkable desktop app serves as a crucial bridge between your reMarkable 2 paper tablet and your computer, enhancing file management, providing a larger screen for reviewing notes, and facilitating seamless synchronization. This guide details the features and functionalities of the desktop app, empowering you to integrate your reMarkable 2 into your broader digital workflow.

I. Installing and Setting Up the Desktop App:

1. **Download the App:** Visit the official reMarkable website ([invalid URL removed]) and download the desktop app for your operating system (Windows or macOS).

2. **Install the App:** Run the downloaded installer and follow the on-screen instructions to install the app.

3. **Launch the App:** Once installed, launch the reMarkable desktop app.

4. **Sign In:** You'll be prompted to sign in using your reMarkable account credentials (the same email address and password you use on your reMarkable 2).

II. Key Features and Functionalities:

The reMarkable desktop app offers several key features:

- **File Synchronization:** The app automatically synchronizes your notebooks, PDFs, and ebooks between your reMarkable 2 and your computer via the reMarkable cloud. This ensures that your files are always up-to-date on both devices.
- **File Management:** The app provides a convenient interface for managing your files. You can:
    - **View your files:** Browse through your notebooks, folders, and documents in a list or grid view.
    - **Create folders:** Create new folders to organize your files.
    - **Rename files and folders:** Rename existing files and folders.

- **Delete files and folders:** Delete files and folders (changes will be synced to your reMarkable).
- **Search your notes (Converted to text):** Search within your notes for keywords and phrases. Note that you can only search within text that has been converted from handwriting.

- **Importing Files:** As described in the previous guide on importing files, the desktop app provides the easiest way to import PDFs and EPUBs to your reMarkable 2.
- **Screen Sharing (Live View):** The app allows you to share your reMarkable 2's screen with your computer. This is useful for presentations, online meetings, or screen recording.
- **Offline Access (Limited):** You can access recently opened files even when you're offline. However, changes made offline will not sync until you reconnect to the internet.

III. Using the Desktop App Interface:

The desktop app interface is designed to be intuitive and easy to navigate.

- **Main Window:** The main window displays your files and folders in a similar layout to the "My Files" view on your reMarkable 2.
- **Navigation Panel:** The left-hand panel provides access to different sections:
    - **My Files:** Displays your notebooks, folders, and documents.
    - **Recent:** Shows recently opened files.
- **Toolbar:** The toolbar at the top of the window provides access to key functions:
    - **Import:** Imports files from your computer.
    - **Search:** Searches within your notes.
- **Context Menus (Right-Click):** Right-clicking on a file or folder opens a context menu with options like "Rename," "Delete," and "Move."

IV. Using Screen Sharing (Live View) (What to Click):

1. **Connect Your reMarkable 2:** Ensure that your reMarkable 2 is turned on and connected to the internet (via Wi-Fi).

2. **Open the Desktop App:** Launch the reMarkable desktop app and ensure you are signed in.

3. **Select Your reMarkable 2:** If you have multiple reMarkable devices connected to your account, select the one you want to share the screen from.

4. **Click "Live View":** Click the "Live View" button (it may be labeled "Screen Share" in some versions) in the top right corner of the app window.

5. **Sharing Your Screen:** Your reMarkable 2's screen will now be mirrored in the desktop app window. Any actions you take on your reMarkable 2 will be reflected in real time on your computer screen.

V. Managing Files and Folders:

File and folder management in the desktop app is straightforward:

- **Creating Folders (What to Click):** Click the "+" button in the file list area and select "New Folder".
- **Renaming (What to Right-Click):** Right-click on a file or folder and select "Rename".
- **Deleting (What to Right-Click):** Right-click on a file or folder and select "Delete".
- **Moving Files (Drag and Drop):** Drag and drop files and folders to move them between folders.

VI. Key Benefits of Using the Desktop App:

- **Larger Screen for Reviewing Notes:** Reviewing your notes on a larger computer screen can be more comfortable and efficient, especially for complex diagrams or long documents.
- **Convenient File Management:** Managing your files on your computer can be easier than navigating the reMarkable 2's interface, especially when dealing with a large number of files.
- **Seamless Synchronization:** Automatic synchronization ensures that your files are always up-to-date on both your reMarkable 2 and your computer.
- **Easy Importing:** The drag-and-drop import feature simplifies the process of adding new PDFs and EPUBs to your reMarkable 2.
- **Screen Sharing for Presentations:** The live view feature makes it easy to share your reMarkable 2's screen for presentations or online meetings.

By utilizing the reMarkable desktop app, you can significantly enhance your workflow and integrate your reMarkable 2 more seamlessly into your digital environment. It provides a valuable bridge between the paper-like experience of the reMarkable 2 and the convenience of your computer.

Integrating with cloud services (Google Drive, Dropbox, etc.)

Integrating with cloud services on the reMarkable 2 adds a significant layer of convenience and flexibility to your workflow, allowing you to access and manage your files across multiple devices and platforms. Here's a comprehensive guide to understanding how this integration works.

I. Supported Cloud Services:

The reMarkable 2 currently offers direct integration with the following cloud storage services:

- **Google Drive**
- **Dropbox**
- **OneDrive**

II. Setting Up Cloud Integration (What to Press):

1. **Access the Settings Menu:**

   - Swipe down from the top of the screen to open the Quick Settings menu.
   - Tap the gear icon (Settings) in the top right corner.

2. **Navigate to Integrations:**

   - In the Settings menu, tap on "Integrations."

3. **Accept Terms and Conditions:**

   - You'll be presented with the Terms & Conditions for Integrations. Read them and tap "Confirm" to proceed.

4. **Add Your Cloud Service:**

   - You'll see icons for Google Drive, Dropbox, and OneDrive. Tap "Add" next to the service you want to connect.

5. **Sign In to Your Cloud Account:**

   - You'll be redirected to a web page where you can sign in to your Google Drive, Dropbox, or OneDrive account. Enter your login credentials and grant reMarkable the necessary permissions to access your files.

6. **Optional: Name the Integration:**

   ○ You can give a custom name to the integration (e.g., "Work Drive," "Personal Dropbox"). This is helpful if you connect multiple accounts of the same service. If you wish to skip this, simply tap "Cancel".

7. **Integration Active:** Once you've signed in and granted permissions, your cloud service will be connected to your reMarkable 2.

III. Using Cloud Integration:

Once you've set up the integration, you can access your cloud storage directly from your reMarkable 2.

A. Accessing Your Cloud Storage (What to Press):

1. **Open the Menu:** Tap the three horizontal lines icon in the top left-hand corner of the "My Files" view.

2. **Select Your Cloud Service:** In the sidebar menu that appears, you'll see your connected cloud services listed (e.g., "Google Drive," "Dropbox"). Tap on the service you want to access.

B. Browsing and Importing Files (What to Press):

1. **Navigate Your Cloud Storage:** You can now browse through your folders and files within your connected cloud storage.

2. **Importing Files (What to Press):**

   ○ **Tap and Hold:** Tap and hold on a compatible file (PDF or EPUB) you want to import.
   ○ **Tap "Import":** Tap "Import" in the action bar that appears at the top of the screen.
   ○ **Import Multiple Files:** To select multiple files, tap and hold one file, and then tap on the other files you wish to import. Then tap "Import".

C. Exporting Files to Cloud Storage (What to Press):

You can also upload files from your reMarkable 2 to your connected cloud storage.

1. **Select the File(s):** Tap and hold on the file you want to export. Select multiple files by tapping on other files after the first one has been selected.

2. **Tap "Upload":** Tap "Upload" in the action bar that appears at the top of the screen.

3. **Choose the Destination:** You'll be prompted to choose the destination folder within your cloud storage where you want to upload the file.

IV. Important Considerations:

- **Synchronization vs. File Storage:** The reMarkable 2's cloud integrations are primarily for file storage and transfer, *not* real-time synchronization in the same way that the reMarkable cloud works. Changes you make to a file on your reMarkable 2 will *not* automatically sync back to the original file in your Google Drive or Dropbox. You have to manually upload it.
- **File Compatibility:** Only PDF and EPUB files can be directly imported from cloud services to your reMarkable 2. Other file types will not be visible or importable.
- **Internet Connection:** An active internet connection is required for both importing and exporting files to and from cloud services.
- **Storage Limits:** Your cloud storage limits apply. Importing large files can use up significant storage space in your Google Drive, Dropbox, or OneDrive.
- **Security:** Ensure you trust the reMarkable app with access to your cloud storage account before connecting the integration.

V. Use Cases for Cloud Integration:

- **Accessing Files from Other Devices:** Easily access PDFs and ebooks stored in your cloud storage on your reMarkable 2.
- **Backing Up Your reMarkable Notes:** Upload important notebooks or annotated PDFs to your cloud storage for an additional backup.
- **Sharing Files with Others:** Share files directly from your reMarkable 2 by uploading them to a shared folder in your cloud storage.
- **Working with Files from Your Computer:** Seamlessly transfer files between your computer and your reMarkable 2 without needing to use a USB cable.

By integrating your reMarkable 2 with cloud services, you can create a more connected and efficient workflow, bridging the gap between your digital and paper-like experiences.

CHAPTER 5

Beyond Note-Taking

Beyond Note-Taking explores the versatile nature of the reMarkable 2, demonstrating its capabilities beyond traditional note-taking. This chapter delves into using the device as a digital sketchbook, harnessing its paper-like feel for artistic expression and visual brainstorming. We'll also cover creating custom digital planners and journals, leveraging the reMarkable 2 for personal organization and reflection. Managing to-do lists and tasks will be addressed, showcasing how the device can serve as a powerful productivity tool. We'll also explore its potential for musicians by discussing reading and annotating sheet music. Finally, we'll examine how the reMarkable 2 can be used for presentations, offering a unique and engaging way to share your work. By the end of this chapter, you'll appreciate the reMarkable 2's adaptability and discover new ways to integrate it into your creative and professional workflows.

• *Using the reMarkable 2 as a sketchbook*

The reMarkable 2, with its paper-like feel and responsive Marker, offers a compelling experience for artists and sketchers. This guide explores how to leverage the device as a digital sketchbook, covering the available tools, techniques, and tips for maximizing your creative potential.

I. Setting Up Your Digital Sketchbook:

1. **Creating a New Notebook:** Start by creating a new notebook specifically for your sketches.
   - Tap the "+" button on the "My Files" screen.
   - Select "New notebook."
   - Choose a suitable template. The "Blank" template provides a completely free canvas, while the "Dotted" template offers subtle guidance.
   - Name your notebook (e.g., "Sketchbook," "Daily Doodles").

II. Exploring the Drawing Tools:

The reMarkable 2 offers a range of tools that cater to different sketching styles.

- **1. Pencil Tool (What to Press):**

- ○ **Icon:** A pencil tip.
- ○ **Characteristics:** Mimics the feel of a graphite pencil, with varying levels of shading based on pressure and tilt (with the Marker Plus). This is excellent for sketching light outlines, shading, and creating textured effects.
- ○ **Adjusting Thickness (What to Press):** Tap the pencil icon again to adjust the "lead" thickness.
- **2. Pen Tool (What to Press):**

  - ○ **Icon:** A pen nib.
  - ○ **Characteristics:** Provides clean, consistent lines, ideal for line art, outlining, and more defined drawings.
  - ○ **Pen Types (What to Press):** Tapping the pen icon again reveals different pen types:
    - ■ **Ballpoint Pen:** Creates a smooth, consistent line.
    - ■ **Fineliner:** Offers a finer, more precise line.
    - ■ **Marker Pen:** Creates a bolder line, useful for thicker outlines or filling in larger areas.
    - ■ **Calligraphy Pen:** Creates lines that vary in thickness depending on the angle and pressure of the Marker (especially effective with the Marker Plus), ideal for expressive linework.
  - ○ **Adjusting Thickness and Color (What to Press):** Tap the pen icon again to adjust the line thickness and color (black, gray, white).
- **3. Marker Tool (What to Press):**

  - ○ **Icon:** A marker tip.
  - ○ **Characteristics:** Creates broad, semi-transparent strokes, ideal for highlighting, shading, and creating quick washes of color.
  - ○ **Adjusting Thickness and Color (What to Press):** Tap the marker icon again to adjust the thickness and color.

III. Sketching Techniques:

- **Light Sketching:** Start with light pencil strokes to establish the basic composition and proportions of your drawing.
- **Building Up Detail:** Gradually add more detail using darker pencil strokes or the pen tool.
- **Shading:** Use the pencil or marker tool to create shading and add depth to your drawings. Experiment with different levels of pressure and the tilt sensitivity of the Marker Plus for varied shading effects.

- **Line Weight:** Varying the thickness of your lines can add visual interest and emphasis to your drawings. Use thicker lines for outlines and thinner lines for details.
- **Cross-Hatching:** Use intersecting lines to create shading and texture.
- **Hatching:** Use parallel lines to create shading and texture.
- **Blending:** While the reMarkable 2 doesn't have a dedicated blending tool like traditional art software, you can achieve a blending effect by using light pressure with the pencil or marker and layering strokes.

IV. Using Layers for Sketching (What to Press):

Layers can be incredibly useful for sketching, especially for more complex drawings.

1. **Open the Layers Menu:** Tap the stacked papers icon in the toolbar.

2. **Add New Layers:** Use layers to separate different elements of your drawing:

   - **Layer 1: Sketch/Rough Outline:** Use this layer for initial sketches and establishing the composition.
   - **Layer 2: Line Art/Outlines:** Use this layer to create clean, defined outlines over your sketch.
   - **Layer 3: Shading/Details:** Use this layer for adding shading, textures, and other details.
3. **Adjust Layer Visibility:** Use the eye icons to hide or show layers as needed. This allows you to focus on specific elements of your drawing without being distracted by others.

V. Zoom and Navigation:

- **Pinch-to-Zoom:** Use pinch-to-zoom gestures to zoom in for detailed work or zoom out for a broader view.
- **Two-Finger Pan:** When zoomed in, use two fingers to drag the page around.

VI. Importing Images for Tracing or Reference:

You can import images as PDFs to use as references or for tracing.

1. **Import the Image as a PDF:** Convert the image to a PDF file on your computer and then import it to your reMarkable 2.

2. **Create a New Layer:** Create a new layer on top of the imported image.

3. **Trace or Sketch Over the Image:** Use the drawing tools to trace or sketch over the image on the new layer.

4. **Hide or Delete the Image Layer:** Once you're finished, you can hide or delete the image layer.

VII. Tips and Tricks for Sketching on the reMarkable 2:

- **Experiment with Different Tools and Settings:** Try out different pen types, thicknesses, and colors to find what works best for your style.
- **Use Quick Gestures:** Practice using the undo/redo gestures (two-finger tap for undo, three-finger tap for redo) to quickly correct mistakes.
- **Use the Eraser Effectively:** The stroke eraser can be useful for quickly removing entire lines or shapes.
- **Practice Regularly:** As with any artistic skill, practice is key to improving your sketching abilities on the reMarkable 2.

The reMarkable 2 provides a unique and enjoyable digital sketching experience that closely mimics traditional media. By understanding the available tools and techniques, you can unlock its full potential and use it as a powerful tool for your creative endeavors.

- *Creating digital planners and journals*

The reMarkable 2's paper-like feel and flexible tools make it an excellent platform for creating personalized digital planners and journals. This guide explores how to design and utilize these tools for effective organization, goal setting, and personal reflection.

I. Choosing a Template or Creating Your Own:

The foundation of your digital planner or journal is the template. You have two main options: using pre-made templates or creating your own.

A. Using Pre-Made Templates:

The reMarkable 2 comes with some built-in planner templates. These provide basic layouts for daily, weekly, and monthly planning.

1. **Create a New Notebook:** Tap the "+" button on the "My Files" screen and select "New notebook."

2. **Select a Planner Template:** Browse the template options and choose a planner template that suits your needs.

B. Creating Custom Templates (Advanced):

For a truly personalized experience, you can create your own templates using image editing software on your computer (like Photoshop, GIMP, or even Canva).

1. **Design Your Template:** Create an image file (PNG or SVG) with your desired layout. Consider elements like:

   - **Daily/Weekly/Monthly Layouts:** Design sections for appointments, tasks, notes, and goals.
   - **Habit Trackers:** Include spaces for tracking daily or weekly habits.
   - **Gratitude Logs:** Add sections for recording things you are grateful for.
   - **Prompts and Questions:** Include journaling prompts or questions to guide your reflections.

2. **Convert to PDF:** Save your image as a PDF file.

3. **Import the PDF to Your reMarkable 2:** Import the PDF using the reMarkable desktop or mobile app.

II. Setting Up Your Planner/Journal:

1. **Create a New Notebook:** If using a pre-made template, you've already created the notebook. If using a custom template, create a new notebook and select your imported PDF as the template.

2. **Naming Your Planner/Journal:** Give your planner or journal a descriptive name (e.g., "2024 Planner," "Gratitude Journal," "Project Journal").

III. Using the Writing Tools for Planning and Journaling:

The reMarkable 2's writing tools offer flexibility for different planning and journaling styles.

- **Pen Tool:** Use the pen tool for writing appointments, tasks, notes, and journal entries. Different pen types (fineliner, ballpoint, etc.) allow you to vary your writing style.

- **Marker Tool:** Use the marker tool for highlighting important tasks, marking completed items, or adding visual emphasis.
- **Pencil Tool:** Use the pencil tool for sketching, brainstorming, or adding subtle details.

IV. Organizing Your Planner/Journal:

- **Using Pages:** Each page in your notebook can represent a day, week, month, or a specific topic, depending on your chosen template and planning style.
- **Adding Pages (What to Press):** To add a new page, tap the three vertical dots icon (More options) in the toolbar and select "Add Page".
- **Navigation:** Use the page overview (accessed by pinching inwards on the screen) to quickly navigate between pages.

V. Advanced Techniques for Planners and Journals:

- **Creating Checklists:** Manually draw checkboxes next to tasks or use the Checklists template.
- **Using Layers:** Use layers to separate different types of information or to create reusable elements (e.g., a weekly habit tracker that you can copy to each weekly page).
- **Color-Coding:** Use different colors to categorize tasks, appointments, or journal entries.
- **Date/Time Stamps:** Manually write the date and time for appointments or journal entries.

VI. Specific Examples:

- **Daily Planner:** Use a daily template with sections for appointments, to-do lists, and notes.
- **Weekly Planner:** Use a weekly template with sections for weekly goals, appointments, and tasks.
- **Monthly Planner:** Use a monthly template with a calendar view and space for monthly goals and notes.
- **Gratitude Journal:** Use a blank or lined template with prompts for recording things you are grateful for each day.
- **Project Journal:** Use a blank or lined template to track progress on specific projects, record ideas, and take meeting notes.

VII. Key Benefits of Using the reMarkable 2 for Planners and Journals:

- **Paper-Like Experience:** The natural writing feel makes planning and journaling more enjoyable and engaging.

- **Distraction-Free Environment:** The lack of notifications and other distractions promotes focus and concentration.
- **Portability:** Carry all your plans and journals in one lightweight device.
- **Organization:** Keep all your plans and journals in one place, easily accessible and searchable.
- **Customization:** Create personalized templates and layouts to suit your specific needs.

Managing to-do lists and tasks

This guide explores various methods for managing your tasks on the reMarkable 2.

I. Creating Simple To-Do Lists:

The most straightforward way to manage tasks is by creating simple lists within a notebook.

1. **Create a New Notebook (or Use an Existing One):** You can dedicate a notebook specifically to to-do lists or keep them within a general notebook.

2. **Choose Your Tool:** Use the pen, marker, or pencil tool. The fineliner pen is often a good choice for clear, readable text.

3. **Write Your Tasks:** Write each task on a separate line.

4. **Add Checkboxes (Manual):** Manually draw small squares or circles next to each task to serve as checkboxes.

5. **Mark Tasks as Complete:** Once a task is finished, you can:

   ○ **Check the Box:** Fill in the manually drawn checkbox with your pen.
   ○ **Cross Out the Task:** Draw a line through the completed task.

II. Using the Checklists Template:

The reMarkable 2 includes a dedicated "Checklists" template that provides pre-made checkboxes.

1. **Create a New Notebook (or Change Template):** When creating a new notebook, select the "Checklists" template. If you want to change the template of an existing notebook, tap the three vertical dots icon (More options) in the

toolbar and select "Change template."

2. **Write Your Tasks:** Write your tasks next to the pre-made checkboxes.

3. **Check Off Tasks:** Tap the checkboxes with your pen to mark tasks as complete.

III. Advanced To-Do List Techniques:

- **Prioritizing Tasks:**

  - **Numbering:** Number your tasks in order of priority.
  - **Color-Coding:** Use different colors (if available) to highlight tasks based on priority (e.g., red for urgent, yellow for important, green for less important).
  - **Symbols:** Use symbols like asterisks (*) or exclamation points (!) to mark important or urgent tasks.
- **Categorizing Tasks:**

  - **Headings:** Use headings to group tasks into categories (e.g., "Work," "Personal," "Household").
  - **Tags:** Use tags to categorize tasks across different notebooks (e.g., "Project X," "Meeting Notes," "Follow Up").
- **Using Layers (for Complex Lists):** If you have a complex to-do list with many nested tasks or subtasks, consider using layers to organize them. You could have one layer for main tasks and another layer for subtasks.

- **Creating Recurring Tasks:** Manually rewrite recurring tasks on the appropriate day or use a recurring template that you create yourself.

IV. Integrating with Other Planning Methods:

- **Daily/Weekly Planning:** Integrate your to-do lists with your daily or weekly planner. You can use the reMarkable 2's planner templates or create your own.
- **Kanban Boards (Manual):** You can create a simple Kanban board on the reMarkable 2 by dividing a page into columns (e.g., "To Do," "In Progress," "Done") and moving tasks between the columns using the selection tool.

V. Limitations:

- **No Reminders or Notifications:** The reMarkable 2 does not have built-in reminders or notifications for tasks.
- **No Task Dependencies or Due Dates (Automatic):** You have to manage task dependencies and due dates manually.
- **No Integration with Task Management Apps:** There is no direct integration with popular task management apps like Todoist, Asana, or Trello.

VI. Workarounds and Alternatives:

- **Importing from Task Management Apps:** You can export your to-do lists from other apps as PDFs and import them to your reMarkable 2. This allows you to view and mark off tasks, but changes won't sync back to the original app.
- **Using Templates from External Sources:** Search online for reMarkable templates designed for task management. Some users create and share more advanced templates that include features like daily task breakdowns or weekly overviews.

VII. Key Benefits of Managing Tasks on the reMarkable 2:

- **Focus and Distraction-Free Environment:** The reMarkable 2's minimalist design and lack of notifications help you focus on your tasks without distractions.
- **Natural Writing Experience:** The paper-like feel of the device makes writing and managing tasks more enjoyable and engaging.
- **Portability:** You can carry all your to-do lists and plans in one lightweight device.

While the reMarkable 2 may not replace dedicated task management apps for complex projects, it offers a unique and effective way to manage simple to-do lists and integrate them with your overall planning and note-taking workflow. Its emphasis on a natural writing experience can be particularly beneficial for those who prefer the tactile feel of pen and paper.

• *Reading and annotating sheet music*

The reMarkable 2, with its large, paper-like display and precise writing capabilities, offers a compelling experience for musicians who want to read and annotate sheet music digitally. This guide explores how to effectively use the device for this purpose.

I. Importing Sheet Music:

The reMarkable 2 supports importing sheet music in PDF format, which is the most common format for digital scores.

1. **Obtain Your Sheet Music in PDF Format:** Ensure that your sheet music is saved as a PDF file. Many online resources offer sheet music in this format. You may need to scan physical sheet music to create a PDF.

2. **Import the PDF:** Use one of the following methods to import the PDF to your reMarkable 2:

   - **reMarkable Desktop App (Recommended):** Drag and drop the PDF into the app or use the import function.
   - **reMarkable Mobile App:** Use the import function within the mobile app.
   - **USB Connection:** Connect your reMarkable 2 to your computer via USB and copy the PDF to the "documents" folder.

II. Setting Up Your reMarkable 2 for Sheet Music:

- **Create a Dedicated Notebook (Optional):** You can create a dedicated notebook for your sheet music to keep it organized.
- **Rotate the Device (If Necessary):** Depending on the orientation of your sheet music, you may need to rotate your reMarkable 2 to landscape mode for better viewing. You can lock the rotation in the quick settings menu (swipe down from the top).

III. Annotating Sheet Music:

The reMarkable 2 offers several tools that are useful for annotating sheet music.

- **1. Pen Tool (What to Press):**

  - **Icon:** A pen nib.
  - **Function:** Use this for:
    - **Writing Fingerings:** Add fingerings above or below notes.
    - **Marking Dynamics:** Add dynamic markings (e.g., *p, f, mf*).
    - **Adding Articulation Marks:** Add articulation marks (e.g., staccato, legato).
    - **Making Notes and Comments:** Write notes or comments about the music.
  - **Pen Types:** The fineliner or ballpoint pen is usually best for precise annotations.

- - **Adjusting Thickness and Color:** Adjust the thickness and color of the pen as needed.
- **2. Marker Tool (What to Press):**

  - - **Icon:** A marker tip.
  - - **Function:** Use this for:
    - - **Highlighting Important Sections:** Highlight key passages, phrases, or measures.
    - - **Marking Repeats:** Mark repeat signs or sections.
  - - **Adjusting Thickness and Color:** Adjust the thickness and color of the marker as needed.
- **3. Eraser Tool (What to Press):**

  - - **Icon:** An eraser.
  - - **Function:** Erase any mistakes or unwanted annotations.
  - - **Eraser Options:** Use the stroke eraser for quickly removing entire markings.
- **4. Zoom (What to Press):**

  - - **Icon:** Magnifying glass.
  - - **Function:** Zoom in for detailed work, especially when adding small annotations or working with dense scores. Use pinch-to-zoom for quick zooming.

IV. Advanced Annotation Techniques:

- **Using Layers (What to Press):** Layers can be extremely useful for complex annotations or for separating different types of markings.

  - - **Layer 1: Original Score:** Keep the original sheet music on the background layer.
  - - **Layer 2: Fingerings:** Add fingerings on a separate layer.
  - - **Layer 3: Performance Notes:** Add performance notes, dynamics, and other markings on another layer.
  - - This allows you to easily show or hide specific types of annotations.
- **Creating Custom Symbols:** If you need to use symbols that aren't easily drawn freehand, you can create them in a vector graphics program and import them as PNGs or SVGs to paste onto your score using the selection tool and copy/paste functionality.

V. Organizing Your Sheet Music:

- **Folders:** Create folders for different genres, composers, or instruments.
- **Tags:** Use tags to categorize your sheet music by key, tempo, or other relevant criteria.

VI. Key Benefits of Using the reMarkable 2 for Sheet Music:

- **Paper-Like Experience:** The natural writing feel makes annotating sheet music more intuitive and enjoyable.
- **Large Display:** The 10.3-inch display provides ample space for viewing most scores.
- **Portability:** Carry a large library of sheet music in one lightweight device.
- **No More Photocopies:** Eliminate the need for messy photocopies and bulky binders.
- **Easy Erasing and Editing:** Correct mistakes easily without damaging the original score.

VII. Limitations:

- **Monochrome Display:** The reMarkable 2 has a monochrome display, so you won't be able to see colors in your sheet music or annotations (unless you export with color annotations, which will show up when viewed on a color display).
- **No Automatic Page Turning (Hands-Free):** You have to manually turn pages by swiping or tapping. This can be inconvenient during performance. (However, some third-party accessories provide foot pedals for page turning.)
- **No Audio Playback:** The reMarkable 2 does not have the capability to play audio files.

VIII. Use Cases:

- **Practicing:** Annotate scores with fingerings, dynamics, and other performance notes.
- **Rehearsing:** Mark up rehearsal notes and changes.
- **Performing:** Use the reMarkable 2 as a digital music stand (with the caveat of manual page turns).
- **Teaching:** Annotate scores for students or make notes during lessons.

The reMarkable 2 offers a compelling digital solution for musicians who want to read and annotate sheet music. While it has some limitations, its paper-like feel, large display, and annotation capabilities make it a valuable tool for practice, rehearsal, and performance.

While the reMarkable 2 isn't a traditional presentation device like a tablet running PowerPoint or Keynote, its unique paper-like feel and screen sharing capabilities offer a distinct and engaging way to present information. This guide explores how to leverage the reMarkable 2 for presentations, highlighting its strengths and addressing its limitations.

I. Preparing Your Presentation Content:

There are two primary ways to prepare content for presentations on the reMarkable 2:

A. Creating Content Directly on the reMarkable 2:

- **Create a New Notebook:** You can create a dedicated notebook for your presentation.
- **Use Different Pages for Slides:** Each page in the notebook can serve as a separate slide.
- **Use the Drawing Tools:** Use the pen, marker, and pencil tools to create your presentation content. You can:
  - **Write Key Points:** Write bullet points, headings, and other text.
  - **Draw Diagrams and Charts:** Create visual aids to illustrate your points.
  - **Sketch Ideas:** Quickly sketch out concepts or ideas during your presentation.
- **Import Images (as PDFs):** You can import images as PDFs to include them in your presentation. This is the only way to have images show up on the reMarkable itself.

B. Preparing Content in Other Applications and Importing:

- **Create Slides in PowerPoint, Google Slides, or Keynote:** Create your presentation slides in your preferred presentation software.
- **Export as PDF:** Export your presentation as a PDF file.
- **Import the PDF to Your reMarkable 2:** Import the PDF using the reMarkable desktop or mobile app.

II. Presenting with the reMarkable 2:

There are two main ways to present using the reMarkable 2:

A. Using Live View (Screen Sharing):

This is the most effective way to present using the reMarkable 2.

1. **Connect Your reMarkable 2 and Computer:** Ensure both your reMarkable 2 and your computer are connected to the internet and that you're logged into the same reMarkable account on both devices.

2. **Open the reMarkable Desktop App:** Launch the desktop app on your computer.

3. **Select Your reMarkable 2:** If you have multiple reMarkable devices, select the one you'll be presenting with.

4. **Start Live View (What to Click):** Click the "Live View" button (or "Screen Share" in some versions) in the top right corner of the app.

5. **Present:** Your reMarkable 2's screen will now be mirrored on your computer screen. You can use your Marker to write, draw, and navigate through your presentation. The audience will see everything you do on your reMarkable 2 on the shared screen.

B. Presenting Directly from the reMarkable 2 (Without Screen Sharing):

This method is less ideal for formal presentations to large audiences but can be useful for smaller group discussions or informal settings.

1. **Open Your Notebook or PDF:** Open the notebook or PDF containing your presentation content.

2. **Navigate Between Pages:** Use swipes or taps to navigate between pages.

3. **Present:** You can then show the reMarkable 2 screen directly to your audience.

III. Advantages of Using the reMarkable 2 for Presentations:

- **Natural Writing and Drawing Experience:** The paper-like feel and low latency of the Marker provide a very natural and engaging way to present information.

- **Focus and Distraction-Free:** The reMarkable 2's minimalist design and lack of notifications help you stay focused on your presentation.
- **Interactive Presentations:** You can actively write, draw, and annotate during your presentation, making it more interactive and dynamic.
- **Unique and Memorable:** Using the reMarkable 2 for presentations offers a unique and memorable experience for your audience.

IV. Limitations of Using the reMarkable 2 for Presentations:

- **Monochrome Display:** The reMarkable 2 has a monochrome display, so you cannot present in color. Color annotations will only appear when exported.
- **No Animations or Transitions:** You cannot use animations, transitions, or other dynamic effects like in traditional presentation software.
- **No Audio or Video Playback:** The reMarkable 2 does not support audio or video playback.
- **Dependence on Screen Sharing for Larger Audiences:** For larger audiences, screen sharing via the desktop app is essential. This requires a stable internet connection for both your reMarkable 2 and your computer.
- **Manual Page Turns:** You have to manually turn pages, which can be slightly less convenient than using a clicker.

V. Tips for Effective Presentations with the reMarkable 2:

- **Keep it Simple:** Focus on clear and concise visuals and text. The monochrome display and lack of animations encourage a simpler presentation style.
- **Use Large Font Sizes:** Ensure that your text is large enough to be easily read by your audience, especially if you're using screen sharing.
- **Practice Your Presentation:** Practice your presentation beforehand to ensure a smooth flow and familiarize yourself with navigating between pages and using the drawing tools.
- **Use a Stand (Optional):** A stand can help position your reMarkable 2 for better visibility during presentations.
- **Test Your Setup:** Before your presentation, test your screen sharing setup to ensure that everything is working correctly.

VI. Use Cases:

- **Brainstorming Sessions:** The reMarkable 2 is excellent for brainstorming sessions, allowing you to capture ideas and visualize concepts in real time.
- **Design Reviews:** You can use the reMarkable 2 to annotate design mockups or provide feedback on visual materials.

- **Online Meetings and Webinars:** The screen sharing feature allows you to share your notes and drawings during online meetings or webinars.
- **Teaching and Training:** The reMarkable 2 can be used to deliver interactive lessons or training sessions.

The reMarkable 2 offers a unique and engaging way to present information, particularly in situations where a natural writing and drawing experience is beneficial. While it has some limitations compared to traditional presentation software, its strengths make it a valuable tool for certain types of presentations and interactive discussions.

CHAPTER 6

Customization and Settings

Customization and Settings delves into the various ways you can personalize and optimize your reMarkable 2 experience. This chapter guides you through adjusting device settings to match your preferences, including display and power management for optimal battery life. We'll cover essential aspects of managing storage and backups, ensuring your valuable notes and documents are safe and accessible. The process of updating the reMarkable 2 software to access new features and improvements will also be explained. Finally, we'll address troubleshooting common issues, providing practical solutions to keep your device running smoothly. By the end of this chapter, you'll have a comprehensive understanding of how to configure your reMarkable 2 to best suit your individual needs and maintain its optimal performance.

• *Personalizing your device settings*

The reMarkable 2 offers a range of customizable settings that allow you to tailor the device to your individual preferences and workflow. This comprehensive guide will walk you through the various settings options, explaining their functions and how to adjust them for an optimized experience.

I. Accessing the Settings Menu (What to Press):

1. **Swipe Down:** Swipe down from the top of the screen to open the Quick Settings menu.

2. **Tap the Gear Icon:** Tap the gear icon (Settings) located in the top right corner of the Quick Settings menu.

II. Navigating the Settings Menu:

The Settings menu is organized into several categories. You navigate by tapping on the category names.

III. Key Settings Categories and Options:

A. General:

- **About:** Displays information about your reMarkable 2, including the model, serial number, and software version. This is useful for troubleshooting or contacting reMarkable support.
- **Wi-Fi:** Manage your Wi-Fi connections. You can connect to new networks, disconnect from existing networks, and view network details.
  - **What to Press:** Tap on "Wi-Fi" to access the Wi-Fi settings.
  - **Connecting to a Network:** Tap on a network name, enter the password if required, and tap "Connect."
- **Handwriting conversion:** Manage handwriting conversion settings.
  - **What to Press:** Tap on "Handwriting conversion" to access the settings.
  - **Handwriting conversion:** Toggle the switch to enable or disable the feature.
  - **Language:** Select the language that the remarkable will use when converting your handwriting to text.
- **Storage:** Displays information about your device's storage usage.
  - **What to Press:** Tap on "Storage" to view the storage usage.
  - **Used Space:** Shows how much storage space is currently being used by your notebooks, PDFs, and other files.
  - **Free Space:** Shows how much storage space is available.
- **Legal:** Contains legal information, including terms of service and privacy policy.

B. Display:

- **Brightness:** Adjust the screen brightness.
  - **What to Press:** Tap on "Display" to access display settings.
  - **Brightness Slider:** Drag the slider to the left to decrease brightness and to the right to increase it.
- **Dark mode:** Toggle dark mode on or off. Dark Mode changes the UI and some templates to a darker colour scheme.
  - **What to Press:** Tap on the switch to toggle dark mode.

C. Power:

- **Sleep mode:** Adjust the time before the device automatically enters sleep mode. This helps conserve battery life.
  - **What to Press:** Tap on "Power" to access power settings.
  - **Select a Time:** Choose a time interval from the available options (e.g., 1 minute, 5 minutes, 15 minutes, Never).
- **Power off:** Completely power off the device.
  - **What to Press:** Tap on "Power off" to turn off the device.

D. Input:

- **Handwriting settings:** Adjust settings related to handwriting input.
  - **What to Press:** Tap on "Input" to access input settings.
  - **Palm rejection:** Toggle palm rejection on or off. This feature prevents accidental markings from your palm touching the screen while writing.
  - **Tilt sensitivity:** Adjust the tilt sensitivity of the Marker Plus (if you have one). This affects how the line thickness and shading change based on the angle of the Marker.
    - **What to Press:** Tap on "Tilt sensitivity" to access tilt settings.
    - **Sensitivity slider:** Drag the slider to adjust the sensitivity.
- **Touch input:** Toggle touch input on or off. When touch input is off, you can only interact with the screen using the Marker.
  - **What to Press:** Tap on the switch to toggle touch input.

E. Integrations:

- **Cloud Services (Google Drive, Dropbox, OneDrive):** Manage your connected cloud storage accounts.
  - **What to Press:** Tap on "Integrations" to access integration settings.
  - **Adding a Service:** Tap "Add" next to the service you want to connect and follow the on-screen prompts to sign in.
  - **Removing a Service:** Tap on the connected service and select "Remove."
  - **Renaming a Service:** Tap on the connected service and select "Rename."

F. Account:

- **Account details:** View your reMarkable account information.
  - **What to Press:** Tap on "Account" to access account details.
  - **Email address:** Shows the email address associated with your reMarkable account.
  - **Change password:** Allows you to change your reMarkable account password.
  - **Sign out:** Signs you out of your reMarkable account on the device.
- **Device security:** Manage device security settings.
  - **What to Press:** Tap on "Device security" to access device security settings.
  - **Screen lock:** Set up a screen lock to require a PIN or password to unlock your reMarkable 2.
    - **What to Press:** Tap on "Screen lock" to set up a screen lock.

- **Choose a PIN or Password:** Follow the on-screen instructions to set up a PIN or password.

G. Software:

- **Software update:** Check for and install software updates for your reMarkable 2.
  - **What to Press:** Tap on "Software" to access software settings.
  - **Check for updates:** Tap on "Check for updates" to see if any new software versions are available.
  - **Install updates:** If an update is available, tap on "Install" to begin the update process.

IV. Personalization Tips:

- **Brightness:** Adjust the brightness to suit your environment. Lower brightness conserves battery life.
- **Sleep Mode:** Set a shorter sleep mode time to conserve battery life if you frequently set your reMarkable 2 down for short periods.
- **Palm Rejection:** Ensure palm rejection is enabled to prevent accidental markings.
- **Dark Mode:** Use dark mode if you prefer a darker interface or find it easier on your eyes in low-light conditions.

By exploring and adjusting these settings, you can create a personalized reMarkable 2 experience that perfectly matches your preferences and enhances your productivity and creativity. Regularly checking for software updates is also recommended to ensure you have the latest features and improvements.

• Adjusting display and power settings

The reMarkable 2's display and power settings are crucial for both user comfort and maximizing battery life. This comprehensive guide will explain each setting in detail, providing practical advice on how to configure them for various use cases.

I. Accessing Display and Power Settings (What to Press):

Both display and power settings are accessed through the main Settings menu:

1. **Swipe Down:** Swipe down from the top of the screen to open the Quick Settings menu.
2. **Tap the Gear Icon:** Tap the gear icon (Settings) located in the top right corner of the Quick Settings menu.

3. **Navigate to Display or Power:** In the Settings menu, tap either "Display" or "Power" to access the respective settings.

II. Display Settings:

The display settings primarily control the screen's brightness and appearance.

A. Brightness (What to Press):

The brightness setting controls the intensity of the light emitted by the reMarkable 2's display.

1. **Access Display Settings:** Follow the steps above to access the Display settings.

2. **Adjust the Brightness Slider (What to Press):** A horizontal slider is used to adjust the brightness level.

   - **Drag Left:** Drag the slider to the left to decrease the brightness, making the screen dimmer.
   - **Drag Right:** Drag the slider to the right to increase the brightness, making the screen brighter.

Practical Considerations for Brightness:

- **Indoor Use:** In most indoor environments, a lower brightness setting is sufficient and will conserve battery life.
- **Outdoor Use:** In bright outdoor conditions, you'll need to increase the brightness to ensure good screen visibility. However, be aware that this will consume more battery power.
- **Eye Strain:** Adjust the brightness to a level that is comfortable for your eyes and minimizes eye strain, especially during prolonged use.
- **Ambient Light:** Consider the ambient lighting conditions when adjusting brightness. In darker environments, a lower brightness setting is preferable.

B. Dark Mode (What to Press):

Dark mode inverts the color scheme of the reMarkable 2's interface, displaying a dark background with light text and icons.

1. **Access Display Settings:** Follow the steps above to access the Display settings.

2. **Toggle Dark Mode (What to Press):** Tap the toggle switch next to "Dark mode" to enable or disable it.

   - **Enabled:** The interface will switch to a dark color scheme.
   - **Disabled:** The interface will use the standard light color scheme.

Practical Considerations for Dark Mode:

- **Low-Light Environments:** Dark mode can be more comfortable for viewing in low-light environments, reducing eye strain.
- **Battery Life (Minimal Effect):** While some devices with OLED screens see significant battery savings with dark mode, the reMarkable 2 uses an E Ink display, which consumes very little power when displaying static images. The battery savings from dark mode on the reMarkable 2 are minimal.
- **Personal Preference:** Ultimately, the choice of whether to use dark mode is a matter of personal preference.

III. Power Settings:

The power settings are primarily focused on managing battery usage.

A. Sleep Mode (What to Press):

Sleep mode puts the reMarkable 2 into a low-power state when it's not in use, conserving battery life.

1. **Access Power Settings:** Follow the steps above to access the Power settings.

2. **Select a Sleep Mode Time (What to Press):** Tap on "Sleep mode."

3. **Choose a Time Interval:** Select a time interval from the available options:

   - **1 minute:** The device will enter sleep mode after 1 minute of inactivity.
   - **5 minutes:** The device will enter sleep mode after 5 minutes of inactivity.
   - **15 minutes:** The device will enter sleep mode after 15 minutes of inactivity.
   - **Never:** The device will not automatically enter sleep mode.

Practical Considerations for Sleep Mode:

- **Battery Life vs. Convenience:** A shorter sleep mode time (e.g., 1 minute) will conserve battery life more effectively but may require you to wake the device more frequently. A longer sleep mode time (e.g., 15 minutes) is more convenient but will consume more battery power.

- **Frequent Use:** If you use your reMarkable 2 frequently throughout the day, a longer sleep mode time or even setting it to "Never" might be more suitable.
- **Infrequent Use:** If you use your reMarkable 2 less frequently, a shorter sleep mode time is recommended to maximize battery life.

B. Power Off (What to Press):

Powering off completely shuts down the reMarkable 2, preventing any battery drain.

1. **Access Power Settings:** Follow the steps above to access the Power settings.

2. **Tap "Power off" (What to Press):** Tap the "Power off" option.

3. **Confirm Power Off:** A confirmation prompt will appear. Tap "Power off" again to confirm.

Practical Considerations for Powering Off:

- **Long Periods of Non-Use:** If you are not planning to use your reMarkable 2 for an extended period, it's best to power it off completely to conserve battery life.
- **Troubleshooting:** Powering off and then turning the device back on can sometimes resolve minor software glitches or performance issues.

IV. Optimizing Battery Life:

Here are some additional tips for extending your reMarkable 2's battery life:

- **Lower Brightness:** As mentioned earlier, reducing the screen brightness is one of the most effective ways to conserve battery power.
- **Short Sleep Mode Time:** Set a shorter sleep mode time to minimize battery drain when the device is not in use.
- **Disable Wi-Fi When Not Needed:** If you don't need to sync files or access online services, disable Wi-Fi to conserve battery life.
- **Avoid Extreme Temperatures:** Avoid exposing your reMarkable 2 to extreme temperatures, as this can negatively affect battery performance.
- **Keep Software Updated:** Regularly updating your reMarkable 2's software can often include battery life optimizations.

V. Summary of Display and Power Settings:

Setting	Function	Impact on Battery Life
Brightness	Controls screen illumination.	Higher = More Drain
Dark Mode	Inverts the interface colors.	Minimal
Sleep Mode	Automatically puts the device into a low-power state after a period of inactivity.	Shorter Time = Less Drain
Power Off	Completely shuts down the device.	No Drain

By understanding and adjusting these display and power settings, you can optimize your reMarkable 2 for both comfortable viewing and extended battery life, ensuring a seamless and productive digital paper experience.

- *Managing storage and backups*

Managing storage and ensuring regular backups are crucial for protecting your valuable notes, documents, and creative work on the reMarkable 2. This guide provides a comprehensive overview of how to manage storage space and implement effective backup strategies.

I. Understanding Storage on the reMarkable 2:

The reMarkable 2 has internal storage that is used to store your notebooks, PDFs, ebooks, and other files. It's important to monitor your storage usage to avoid running out of space.

A. Checking Storage Usage (What to Press):

1. **Access the Settings Menu:** Swipe down from the top of the screen to open the Quick Settings menu and tap the gear icon (Settings).
2. **Navigate to Storage:** In the Settings menu, tap "Storage."
3. **View Storage Information:** The Storage screen displays:
   - **Used Space:** The total amount of storage currently in use.
   - **Free Space:** The amount of storage space still available.

B. Factors Affecting Storage Usage:

- **Notebooks:** The size of your notebooks depends on the number of pages, the complexity of your handwriting, and the use of images or other embedded content.
- **PDFs and Ebooks:** The size of PDF and ebook files varies depending on the number of pages, image resolution, and other factors. Large, image-heavy PDFs can consume significant storage space.
- **Templates:** Custom templates do take up space, so if you have a lot of custom templates, this can also add up.

II. Managing Storage Space:

If you're running low on storage space, you can take the following steps:

A. Deleting Unnecessary Files (What to Press):

1. **Go to the "My Files" View:** Navigate to the main "My Files" screen.
2. **Select the File(s):** Tap and hold on the notebook, PDF, or ebook you want to delete until a checkmark appears. You can select multiple files by tapping on other items.
3. **Tap the Trash Can Icon:** Tap the trash can icon in the top bar.
4. **Confirm Deletion:** Confirm that you want to delete the selected files.

B. Removing Unused Templates:

Removing custom templates you no longer use can free up some space. This is done by deleting the PDF files you imported as templates.

C. Optimizing PDF Files (Before Importing):

Before importing large PDFs, you can optimize them on your computer to reduce their file size. Several PDF optimization tools are available online and offline. This can significantly reduce the storage space they require on your reMarkable 2.

III. Backup Strategies:

Regular backups are essential to protect your data in case of device malfunction, loss, or accidental deletion. The reMarkable 2 offers several backup options:

A. reMarkable Cloud Sync:

This is the primary and most convenient backup method.

1. **Automatic Sync:** By default, your reMarkable 2 automatically synchronizes your notebooks and documents to the reMarkable cloud when connected to Wi-Fi.
2. **Accessing Your Files on Other Devices:** You can access your synced files using the reMarkable desktop and mobile apps.

Benefits of reMarkable Cloud Sync:

- **Automatic:** Backups happen automatically in the background.
- **Cross-Device Access:** Access your files on your computer, smartphone, or other devices.
-
- **Version History (Limited):** reMarkable keeps some version history of your documents, allowing you to revert to earlier versions in some cases.

B. Exporting Files (Manual Backup):

You can manually export your notebooks and PDFs as PDF, PNG, or SVG files and store them on your computer or other storage devices. This provides an additional layer of backup.

1. **Open the Notebook or PDF:** Open the file you want to export.
2. **Access the More Options Menu:** Tap the three vertical dots icon (More options) in the toolbar.
3. **Select "Export PDF", "Export PNG" or "Export SVG":** Choose the desired export format.
4. **Send the Exported File:** Save the exported file to your computer, an external hard drive, or cloud storage service (like Google Drive or Dropbox).
5.

C. Connecting to Cloud Services (Google Drive, Dropbox, OneDrive):

While not a direct backup in the same way as reMarkable's cloud, connecting to other cloud storage services also provides a way to have your files stored elsewhere.

1. **Connect to Your Cloud Service:** Follow the instructions in the "Integrating with cloud services" guide to connect your reMarkable 2 to your Google Drive, Dropbox, or OneDrive account.

2. **Upload Files to Your Cloud Storage:** Manually upload important notebooks or PDFs to your connected cloud storage.

IV. Best Practices for Storage and Backups:

- **Regularly Check Storage Usage:** Monitor your storage usage to avoid running out of space.
- **Delete Unnecessary Files:** Delete files you no longer need to free up storage space.
- **Rely on reMarkable Cloud Sync:** Ensure that cloud sync is enabled and that your reMarkable 2 is regularly connected to Wi-Fi to ensure automatic backups.
- **Export Important Files Periodically:** Export important notebooks or PDFs as an extra backup measure.
-
- **Organize Your Files:** Use folders and tags to keep your files organized, making it easier to manage and back them up.
-
- **Test Your Backups:** Periodically test your backups by restoring a file from the reMarkable cloud or from an exported copy to ensure that your backups are working correctly.

By following these guidelines, you can effectively manage storage space on your reMarkable 2 and implement robust backup strategies to protect your valuable work. Combining reMarkable cloud sync with manual exports or cloud service connections will ensure that your data is safe and accessible.

- ## *Updating the reMarkable 2 software*

Keeping your reMarkable 2's software updated is essential for accessing new features, performance improvements, bug fixes, and security enhancements. This guide provides a clear explanation of how to update your device's software.

I. Checking for Updates (What to Press):

1. **Access the Settings Menu:** Swipe down from the top of the screen to open the Quick Settings menu and tap the gear icon (Settings).

2. **Navigate to Software:** In the Settings menu, tap "Software."

3. **Check for Updates (What to Press):** Tap "Check for updates."

II. The Update Process:

If an update is available, your reMarkable 2 will begin downloading it automatically (if you have "Automatic updates" enabled, see below).

1. **Downloading the Update:** The download progress will be displayed on the screen. Ensure your reMarkable 2 is connected to Wi-Fi during the download.

2. **Preparing the Update:** Once the download is complete, the reMarkable 2 will prepare the update for installation.

3. **Installing the Update (What to Press):** You'll be prompted to install the update. Tap "Install" to begin the installation process.

4. **Device Restart:** Your reMarkable 2 will restart automatically to complete the installation. Do not interrupt the restart process.

5. **Update Complete:** Once the restart is complete, your reMarkable 2 will be running the latest software version.

III. Automatic Updates (What to Press):

The reMarkable 2 offers the option to automatically download and install software updates.

1. **Access the Settings Menu:** As described above.

2. **Navigate to Software:** As described above.

3. **Toggle Automatic Updates (What to Press):** If available, you will see a toggle for "Automatic updates". Toggle it on to enable automatic updates.

Benefits of Automatic Updates:

- **Convenience:** You don't have to manually check for updates.
- **Always Up-to-Date:** Ensures that your device is always running the latest software version.

IV. Important Considerations During the Update Process:

- **Wi-Fi Connection:** A stable Wi-Fi connection is required for downloading and installing updates.
- **Battery Level:** Ensure your reMarkable 2 has sufficient battery charge (at least 50% is recommended) before starting an update. Interrupting an update due to low battery can cause problems.
- **Do Not Interrupt the Update:** Do not power off or restart your reMarkable 2 during the update process. This can corrupt the software and require a factory reset.
- **Time Required:** The update process can take several minutes, depending on the size of the update.

V. Troubleshooting Update Issues:

- **Update Download Fails:** Check your Wi-Fi connection and try again. If the problem persists, restart your reMarkable 2.
- **Installation Fails:** If the installation fails, try restarting your reMarkable 2 and attempting the update again. If the issue continues, contact reMarkable support.
- **Device Stuck During Update:** If your reMarkable 2 gets stuck during the update process, try a force restart by holding down the power button for an extended period (around 10-15 seconds). If this doesn't resolve the issue, contact reMarkable support.

VI. Checking Your Current Software Version (What to Press):

You can check your current software version in the Settings menu:

1. **Access the Settings Menu:** As described above.

2. **Navigate to General:** In the Settings menu, tap "General."

3. **Tap About:** Tap "About".

4. **View Software Version:** The software version is displayed on the About screen.

VII. Benefits of Keeping Your Software Up-to-Date:

- **New Features:** Software updates often introduce new features and functionalities.
- **Performance Improvements:** Updates can improve the device's performance, making it faster and more responsive.
- **Bug Fixes:** Updates address bugs and glitches that may be present in previous software versions.
- **Security Enhancements:** Updates can include security patches that protect your device from vulnerabilities.

• Troubleshooting common issues

While the reMarkable 2 is generally a reliable device, users may occasionally encounter issues. This guide addresses some common problems and provides troubleshooting steps to help you resolve them.

I. Connectivity Issues:

A. Wi-Fi Connection Problems:

- **Problem:** Cannot connect to Wi-Fi, unstable connection, or slow internet speeds.
- **Solutions:**
    1. **Check Wi-Fi Network:** Ensure your Wi-Fi network is working correctly and that other devices can connect.
    2. **Restart Your reMarkable 2:** Power off your reMarkable 2 completely and then turn it back on.
    3. **Restart Your Router/Modem:** Restart your Wi-Fi router or modem.
    4. **Check Wi-Fi Password:** Double-check that you are entering the correct Wi-Fi password.
    5. **Move Closer to the Router:** If the signal is weak, move closer to your Wi-Fi router.
    6. **Forget and Reconnect to the Network:** On your reMarkable 2, go to Settings > Wi-Fi, forget the network, and then reconnect to it.

B. Syncing Problems:

- **Problem:** Files are not syncing between your reMarkable 2 and the reMarkable cloud.
- **Solutions:**

1. **Check Internet Connection:** Ensure both your reMarkable 2 and any devices using the reMarkable app (desktop or mobile) have stable internet connections.
2. **Restart Your reMarkable 2:** Power off your reMarkable 2 completely and then turn it back on.
3. **Check reMarkable Cloud Status:** Check the reMarkable status page (if available) to see if there are any reported outages or service disruptions.
4. **Sign Out and Back In:** Sign out of your reMarkable account on both your reMarkable 2 and the apps, and then sign back in.

II. Display and Input Issues:

A. Marker Not Working or Inaccurate Input:

- **Problem:** The Marker is not writing, writing is inconsistent, or the cursor is not tracking accurately.
- **Solutions:**
    1. **Check Marker Tip:** Ensure the Marker tip is properly attached and not damaged. Replace the tip if necessary.
    2. **Restart Your reMarkable 2:** Power off your reMarkable 2 completely and then turn it back on.
    3. **Clean the Screen:** Clean the reMarkable 2's screen with a soft, dry cloth.
    4. **Check for Interference:** Ensure there are no magnets or other sources of electromagnetic interference near the reMarkable 2.
    5. **Contact reMarkable Support:** If the problem persists, the Marker or the reMarkable 2 itself may need to be repaired or replaced.

B. Screen Freezing or Unresponsive:

- **Problem:** The screen freezes, becomes unresponsive to touch or Marker input, or displays a black or white screen.
- **Solutions:**
    1. **Force Restart:** Hold down the power button for an extended period (around 10-15 seconds) until the device restarts.
    2. **Contact reMarkable Support:** If the problem persists after a force restart, contact reMarkable support.

III. Software and Update Issues:

A. Update Download or Installation Fails:

- **Problem:** Software updates fail to download or install.
- **Solutions:**

1. **Check Wi-Fi Connection:** Ensure you have a stable Wi-Fi connection.
2. **Restart Your reMarkable 2:** Power off your reMarkable 2 completely and then turn it back on.
3. **Check reMarkable Servers:** Check the reMarkable status page (if available) to see if there are any reported issues with their servers.
4. **Try Again Later:** Sometimes, server issues can cause temporary problems with updates. Try again later.

B. Device Stuck During Update:

- **Problem:** The reMarkable 2 becomes stuck during the update process.
- **Solutions:**
    1. **Force Restart:** Hold down the power button for an extended period (around 10-15 seconds) until the device restarts.
    2. **Contact reMarkable Support:** If the problem persists after a force restart, contact reMarkable support.

IV. Other Common Issues:

A. Battery Draining Quickly:

- **Problem:** The battery life is significantly shorter than expected.
- **Solutions:**
    1. **Lower Screen Brightness:** Reduce the screen brightness.
    2. **Shorten Sleep Mode Time:** Set a shorter sleep mode time.
    3. **Disable Wi-Fi When Not Needed:** Turn off Wi-Fi when you don't need it.
    4. **Check for Background Processes:** Although less common, if you have very complex documents, they may be causing some background processing.
    5. **Contact reMarkable Support:** If the problem persists, the battery may need to be replaced.

B. Problems with Imported PDFs:

- **Problem:** PDFs are not displaying correctly, fonts are missing, or images are distorted.
- **Solutions:**
    1. **Optimize the PDF:** Use a PDF optimization tool on your computer to reduce the file size and simplify the formatting.

2. **Try a Different PDF Viewer on Your Computer:** If the PDF displays incorrectly in multiple viewers on your computer, the file itself may be corrupted.
3. **Contact reMarkable Support:** If the problem persists, contact reMarkable support with the problematic PDF file.

V. Contacting reMarkable Support:

If you are unable to resolve an issue using these troubleshooting steps, you should contact reMarkable support. You can usually find contact information on their website.

VI. General Tips for Troubleshooting:

- **Restart Your Device:** Restarting your reMarkable 2 is often the first and most effective troubleshooting step.
- **Check the reMarkable Website and Community Forums:** The reMarkable website and community forums can be valuable resources for finding solutions to common problems.
- **Keep Your Software Up-to-Date:** Keeping your reMarkable 2's software updated can often resolve bugs and improve performance.

By following these troubleshooting steps, you can often resolve common issues with your reMarkable 2 and keep it running smoothly. If you encounter a problem that you cannot resolve yourself, don't hesitate to contact reMarkable support for assistance.

CHAPTER 7

<u>Tips and Tricks</u>

Tips and Tricks is dedicated to maximizing your reMarkable 2 experience by uncovering hidden potential and optimizing your workflow. This chapter offers practical advice on extending battery life, ensuring you can rely on your device for longer periods. We'll explore strategies for streamlining your workflow, making your note-taking, sketching, and document management more efficient. We'll also delve into some lesser-known features of the reMarkable 2, revealing hidden gems that can further enhance your productivity. The chapter will also touch upon using third-party accessories to complement your device and expand its functionality. Finally, we'll guide you on joining the reMarkable community, a valuable resource for finding inspiration, sharing tips, and connecting with other users. By the end of this chapter, you'll be equipped with insider knowledge to truly master your reMarkable 2.

- ### *Maximizing battery life*

The reMarkable 2 is known for its impressive battery life, allowing for days of use on a single charge. However, certain usage patterns and settings can affect battery performance.

I. Key Factors Affecting Battery Life:

- **Screen Brightness:** The screen's backlight is the primary power consumer. Higher brightness levels drain the battery faster.
- **Wi-Fi Usage:** Keeping Wi-Fi constantly enabled, especially if the signal is weak or unstable, consumes significant battery power.
- **Sleep Mode Settings:** A longer sleep mode time means the device stays active for longer, draining the battery even when not actively in use.
- **Software Updates:** While updates often include battery optimizations, occasionally a new update might introduce temporary battery drain issues until subsequent patches are released.
- **File Complexity:** Very large or complex documents (especially PDFs with many images) can require more processing power, which can slightly increase battery consumption.
- **Usage Patterns:** Intensive use, such as continuous writing or drawing for extended periods, will naturally drain the battery faster than light use.

II. Strategies for Maximizing Battery Life:

A. Adjusting Display Settings:

- **Lower Brightness:** Reducing the screen brightness is the most effective way to conserve battery power. Use the brightness slider in the Display settings to find a comfortable level that is as low as possible.
  - **What to Press:** Swipe down from the top, tap the gear icon (Settings), tap "Display," and adjust the brightness slider.
- **Use Dark Mode (Minimal Effect):** While dark mode has a significant impact on OLED screens, its effect on the reMarkable 2's E Ink display is minimal. It's primarily a matter of personal preference.
  - **What to Press:** Swipe down from the top, tap the gear icon (Settings), tap "Display," and toggle "Dark mode."

B. Managing Wi-Fi:

- **Disable Wi-Fi When Not Needed:** Turn off Wi-Fi when you're not actively syncing files, downloading updates, or using online services.
  - **What to Press:** Swipe down from the top, tap the Wi-Fi icon to toggle it off. You can also manage Wi-Fi connections in Settings > Wi-Fi.

C. Optimizing Power Settings:

- **Shorten Sleep Mode Time:** Set a shorter sleep mode time to minimize battery drain when the device is idle.
  - **What to Press:** Swipe down from the top, tap the gear icon (Settings), tap "Power," and select a shorter time interval for "Sleep mode."
- **Power Off When Not in Use:** If you're not planning to use your reMarkable 2 for an extended period (e.g., overnight or for several days), power it off completely.
  - **What to Press:** Swipe down from the top, tap the gear icon (Settings), tap "Power," and tap "Power off."

D. Managing Files and Usage Patterns:

- **Avoid Overly Large or Complex PDFs:** While the reMarkable 2 can handle most PDFs, extremely large or complex files can require more processing power. If possible, optimize PDFs on your computer before importing them.
- **Minimize Background Processes:** While the reMarkable 2 doesn't have many background apps running like a traditional tablet, avoid having a huge number of pages open at once. Close notebooks you aren't actively using.
- **Avoid Extreme Temperatures:** Exposing your reMarkable 2 to extreme temperatures (both hot and cold) can negatively affect battery performance.

E. Software and Firmware:

- **Keep Software Updated:** Regularly updating your reMarkable 2's software is important, as updates often include battery life optimizations.
  - **What to Press:** Swipe down from the top, tap the gear icon (Settings), tap "Software," and tap "Check for updates." Consider enabling automatic updates if available.
  -

III. Monitoring Battery Usage:

The reMarkable 2 doesn't provide detailed battery usage statistics like some smartphones or laptops. However, you can generally gauge your battery life based on the battery indicator icon in the top right corner of the screen.

IV. Charging Your reMarkable 2:

- **Use the Included USB-C Cable:** It's recommended to use the USB-C cable that came with your reMarkable 2 for optimal charging.
- **Use a Wall Adapter or Computer USB Port:** You can charge your reMarkable 2 using a wall adapter or by connecting it to a USB port on your computer.
-
- **Charging Time:** It typically takes a few hours to fully charge the reMarkable 2.
-

V. Summary of Battery Saving Tips:

- **Lower Brightness:** Significant impact.
- **Disable Wi-Fi:** Significant impact.
- **Short Sleep Mode:** Moderate impact.
- **Power Off When Not in Use:** Most effective for long-term storage.
- **Optimize PDFs:** Moderate impact, especially for very large files.
- **Keep Software Updated:** Can have a positive impact.

By implementing these strategies, you can significantly extend the battery life of your reMarkable 2 and enjoy uninterrupted use for longer periods. Prioritize reducing screen brightness and managing Wi-Fi usage for the most noticeable improvements.

- *Optimizing your workflow*

The reMarkable 2's unique paper-like experience offers a powerful platform for various workflows, from note-taking and sketching to document review and task management.

This guide provides practical tips and strategies to optimize your workflow and maximize your productivity on the device.

I. Organizing Your Digital Workspace:

Effective organization is crucial for a smooth workflow.

- **Folders:** Use folders to categorize your notebooks and documents. Create a logical folder structure that reflects your needs (e.g., "Work," "Personal," "Projects," "Courses").
- **Tags:** Use tags for more granular organization and cross-referencing. Tags allow you to associate multiple categories with a single file.
- **Naming Conventions:** Use clear and consistent naming conventions for your notebooks and documents to make them easy to find and identify.

II. Streamlining Note-Taking:

- **Templates:** Utilize templates to structure your notes effectively. The reMarkable 2 offers several built-in templates, and you can also create or download custom templates.
- **Layers:** Use layers to separate different elements of your notes or drawings. This allows you to easily edit, move, or hide specific parts without affecting others.
- **Handwriting Conversion:** Convert your handwritten notes to text to make them searchable and easily shareable.
- **Quick Gestures:** Learn and use the quick gestures for undo (two-finger tap), redo (three-finger tap), and other actions to speed up your workflow.

III. Optimizing Document Review:

- **Annotations:** Use the various annotation tools (pen, marker, highlighter) to mark up PDFs and ebooks effectively.
- **Layers for Annotations:** Use layers to separate different types of annotations (e.g., comments, highlights, questions).
- **Zoom and Navigation:** Use zoom and the page overview to navigate through large documents efficiently.

IV. Enhancing Sketching and Drawing:

- **Experiment with Tools:** Explore the different pen types (ballpoint, fineliner, marker, calligraphy) and their settings to find what works best for your style.
- **Use Layers for Complex Drawings:** Use layers to separate different elements of your artwork, making it easier to edit and refine your creations.

- **Import Images for Reference or Tracing:** Import images as PDFs to use as references or for tracing.

V. Managing To-Do Lists and Tasks:

- **Use the Checklists Template:** The built-in Checklists template provides a simple and effective way to manage tasks.
- **Prioritize Tasks:** Use numbering, color-coding, or symbols to prioritize your tasks.
- **Integrate with Daily/Weekly Planning:** Combine your to-do lists with your daily or weekly planning.

VI. Utilizing the Desktop and Mobile Apps:

- **File Management:** Use the desktop app for convenient file management, including creating folders, renaming files, and deleting unnecessary content.
- **Importing and Exporting:** Use the desktop app for efficient importing and exporting of files.
- **Screen Sharing (Live View):** Use the desktop app's Live View feature for presentations or sharing your screen with others.
- **Accessing Notes on Other Devices:** Use the desktop and mobile apps to access your notes and documents on your computer, smartphone, or tablet.

VII. Keyboard Shortcuts (with a connected keyboard):

If you connect a Bluetooth keyboard to your reMarkable 2, you can use keyboard shortcuts for various actions, which can significantly speed up your workflow. The available shortcuts may vary slightly depending on the software version.

VIII. Custom Templates and Community Resources:

- **Explore Custom Templates:** Search online for custom reMarkable templates created by other users. These templates can provide pre-designed layouts for various purposes, such as planners, journals, meeting notes, and more.
- **Join the reMarkable Community:** The reMarkable community forums are a valuable resource for finding tips, tricks, and inspiration from other users.

IX. Specific Workflow Examples:

- **Meeting Notes Workflow:**

    1. Create a dedicated notebook for meeting notes.
    2. Use a meeting notes template.

3. Use the pen tool to take notes during the meeting.
4. Use the marker tool to highlight key action items.
5. Convert handwritten notes to text after the meeting.
6. Share the converted notes via email or export as a PDF.

- **Research Workflow:**

  1. Create a dedicated notebook for each research project.
  2. Import relevant research papers as PDFs.
  3. Use the annotation tools to highlight key findings and add comments.
  4. Use the pen tool to take notes and summarize key information.

- **Sketching Workflow:**

  1. Create a dedicated sketchbook notebook.
  2. Use layers to separate different elements of your drawings.
  3. Experiment with different pen types and settings.
  4. Export your finished artwork as PNG or SVG files.

By implementing these optimization strategies and tailoring your workflow to your specific needs, you can unlock the full potential of your reMarkable 2 and significantly enhance your productivity and efficiency.

• *Exploring hidden features*

Beyond its core functionality, the reMarkable 2 harbors several less obvious features and functionalities that can further enhance your user experience and streamline your workflow. This guide dives into these hidden gems, revealing tips and tricks to help you truly master your device.

I. Quick Gestures and Shortcuts:

- **Undo/Redo:**
  - **Undo (What to Do):** A two-finger tap anywhere on the screen performs an undo action, reversing your last stroke or action.
  - **Redo (What to Do):** A three-finger tap performs a redo action, reapplying an undone action.
- **Quick Menu Access (What to Do):** In some contexts, a long press (tap and hold) on an item or area of the screen may bring up a context-sensitive menu with additional options.

II. Advanced Selection Tool Techniques:

- **Precise Selection:** When using the selection tool (lasso), you don't have to perfectly enclose the items you want to select. The reMarkable 2 is quite good at identifying the intended selection.
- **Copy/Paste Between Notebooks:** You can use the selection tool to copy content from one notebook and paste it into another. This is useful for transferring notes, drawings, or diagrams between different notebooks.
  - **What to Do:** Select the content, tap the selection, and choose "Copy". Then go to the other notebook, tap and hold on the destination page, and select "Paste".

III. Using the USB Web Interface (A Hidden Gem):

This is a somewhat hidden feature that allows you to access your reMarkable 2's file system through a web browser on your computer when connected via USB.

1. **Connect Your reMarkable 2:** Connect your reMarkable 2 to your computer using the USB cable.
2. **Access the IP Address:** On your reMarkable 2, go to Settings > General > About. Note down the IP address displayed.
3. **Open a Web Browser:** On your computer, open a web browser and enter the IP address you noted down in the address bar.
4. **Access Your Files:** You'll be presented with a basic web interface that allows you to browse your reMarkable 2's file system. You can download files (as PDFs) from your reMarkable 2 to your computer using this interface.

Important Notes about the USB Web Interface:

- **Limited Functionality:** This interface is primarily for downloading files. You cannot upload files or perform other file management tasks through it.
- **Potential for Instability:** This feature is not officially advertised or fully supported by reMarkable, so you may encounter occasional bugs or instability.

IV. Template Management:

- **Organizing Templates:** While the reMarkable 2 doesn't have a dedicated template management system, you can organize your custom templates by creating a folder specifically for them.
- **Finding Custom Templates Online:** Many users create and share custom reMarkable templates online. Search online communities and forums to find templates that suit your needs.

V. Using the reMarkable 2 with Third-Party Software (Unofficial):

- **Third-Party Tools and Hacks:** The reMarkable community has developed various unofficial tools and hacks that extend the device's functionality. These tools can offer features like custom launchers, alternative software, and more.
- **Caution:** Using unofficial tools and hacks may void your warranty or cause instability. Proceed with caution and at your own risk.

VI. Exploring the reMarkable Community:

- **reMarkable Community Forum:** The official reMarkable community forum is a valuable resource for finding tips, tricks, and solutions to common problems. You can also connect with other reMarkable users and share your experiences.
- **Other Online Communities:** There are also active reMarkable communities on Reddit and other online platforms.

VII. Specific Examples of Hidden Features in Action:

- **Quickly Moving Content:** Use the selection tool and copy/paste to quickly move a diagram from your notes to a presentation notebook.
- **Downloading Files Without the Desktop App:** If you don't have access to the desktop app on a specific computer, use the USB web interface to download important files.
- **Finding Unique Templates:** Search online communities to find specialized templates for specific tasks, such as project management, habit tracking, or creative writing.
- *Using third-party accessories*

While the reMarkable 2 offers a compelling experience on its own, several third-party accessories can further enhance its functionality, improve ergonomics, and personalize your device. This guide explores some popular third-party accessories and how they can complement your reMarkable 2.

I. Protective Cases and Folios:

- **Purpose:** Protective cases and folios provide protection against scratches, bumps, and other damage. They can also add a touch of style and personalization to your device.
- **Types:**
  - **Folios:** These offer full protection for both the front and back of the reMarkable 2 and often include a built-in stand.
  - **Sleeves:** These provide basic protection against scratches and bumps when storing or transporting your reMarkable 2.
  - **Hard Cases:** These offer more robust protection against impacts.

- **Considerations:** When choosing a case or folio, consider factors like:
  - **Protection Level:** How much protection do you need?
  - **Weight and Bulk:** How much bulk are you willing to add to your device?
  - **Features:** Do you need a built-in stand, pen holder, or other features?
  - **Material and Style:** What material and style do you prefer?

II. Screen Protectors:

- **Purpose:** Screen protectors provide an extra layer of protection against scratches and can also alter the screen's texture.
- **Types:**
  - **Tempered Glass:** Offers the most robust protection against scratches and impacts.
  - **Film Protectors:** Provide basic scratch protection.
  - **Paper-Like Screen Protectors:** These are designed to mimic the texture of paper, providing a more tactile writing experience.
- **Considerations:** If you prioritize the paper-like feel of the reMarkable 2, a paper-like screen protector can enhance that experience. However, some users find that they can wear down Marker tips more quickly.

III. Alternative Markers/Styluses:

- **Purpose:** While the reMarkable 2's Marker is well-designed, some users prefer the feel or features of other styluses.
- **Compatibility:** Not all styluses are compatible with the reMarkable 2's E Ink display technology. It's crucial to choose a stylus that is specifically designed or confirmed to work with the reMarkable 2.
- **Examples:** Some popular alternative styluses include those from Staedtler, Lamy, and other brands.
- **Considerations:** Consider factors like:
  - **Ergonomics:** How comfortable is the stylus to hold?
  - **Tip Type and Feel:** What kind of writing experience do you prefer?
  - **Features:** Does the stylus offer features like tilt sensitivity or an eraser?

IV. Stands and Holders:

- **Purpose:** Stands and holders can improve the ergonomics of using the reMarkable 2, especially for extended writing or drawing sessions.
- **Types:**
  - **Adjustable Stands:** These allow you to adjust the angle of the reMarkable 2 for optimal viewing and writing.
  - **Simple Stands:** These provide a fixed angle for viewing or writing.

- **Considerations:** Consider factors like:
  - **Adjustability:** How adjustable is the stand?
  - **Stability:** How stable is the stand?
  - **Portability:** How portable is the stand?

V. Keyboards:

- **Purpose:** Connecting a Bluetooth keyboard can significantly improve text input speed and efficiency, especially for tasks like writing reports or taking detailed notes.
- **Compatibility:** The reMarkable 2 supports Bluetooth keyboards.
- **Considerations:** Consider factors like:
  - **Size and Portability:** How portable do you need the keyboard to be?
  - **Key Feel:** What kind of typing experience do you prefer?

VI. Other Accessories:

- **USB-C Hubs:** These can expand the reMarkable 2's connectivity, allowing you to connect multiple devices at once.
- **Screen Cleaning Cloths:** A microfiber cloth is essential for keeping your reMarkable 2's screen clean and free of smudges.

VII. Finding Third-Party Accessories:

- **Online Retailers:** Online retailers like Amazon, eBay, and others offer a wide variety of reMarkable 2 accessories.
- **reMarkable Community:** The reMarkable community forums can be a good source for recommendations and reviews of third-party accessories.

VIII. Important Considerations When Choosing Accessories:

- **Compatibility:** Always check for compatibility with the reMarkable 2 before purchasing any third-party accessory.
- **Quality:** Look for accessories from reputable brands or with positive user reviews.
- **Warranty:** Check the warranty offered by the accessory manufacturer.

By carefully selecting and using third-party accessories, you can significantly enhance your reMarkable 2 experience and tailor it to your specific needs and preferences. Whether you're looking for added protection, improved ergonomics, or expanded functionality, there are many options available to help you get the most out of your device.

The reMarkable community is a vibrant and valuable resource for reMarkable 2 users. It's a place to connect with other users, share tips and tricks, find inspiration, get help with troubleshooting, and stay up-to-date on the latest news and developments related to the device.

I. Official reMarkable Channels:

- **reMarkable Website and Blog:** The official reMarkable website ([invalid URL removed]) is the primary source for information about the device, including product updates, software releases, and support documentation. The reMarkable blog often features articles about user workflows, creative uses of the device, and community spotlights.
- **reMarkable Support:** If you encounter technical issues or have questions about your device, the reMarkable support team is available to assist you. You can typically find contact information on their website.

II. reMarkable Community Forum:

The official reMarkable community forum is a dedicated online platform where users can interact with each other and with reMarkable staff.

- **Accessing the Forum:** You can access the forum through the reMarkable website.
- **Creating an Account:** You'll need to create an account to participate in discussions, post questions, and share your work.
- **Forum Sections:** The forum is typically organized into different sections, such as:
  - **General Discussion:** For general conversations about the reMarkable 2.
  - **Tips & Tricks:** For sharing tips and tricks for using the device.
  - **Feature Requests:** For suggesting new features and improvements.
  - **Troubleshooting:** For getting help with technical issues.
  - **Templates:** For sharing and finding custom templates.
  - **Community Showcase:** For sharing your reMarkable creations.
- **Searching the Forum:** Before posting a question, use the forum's search function to see if it has already been answered.
- **Participating in Discussions:** You can participate in existing discussions by replying to posts or create new threads to ask questions or share your own insights.

III. Unofficial reMarkable Communities:

In addition to the official forum, there are several active unofficial reMarkable communities on other platforms:

- **Reddit:** The r/RemarkableTablet subreddit is a popular community on Reddit where users share tips, discuss features, and troubleshoot issues.
- **Facebook Groups:** Several Facebook groups are dedicated to reMarkable users.
- **Other Online Forums and Communities:** You may find reMarkable discussions on other online forums and communities related to technology, productivity, or digital art.

IV. Benefits of Joining the reMarkable Community:

- **Finding Solutions to Problems:** If you encounter a problem with your reMarkable 2, chances are someone else has already experienced it and found a solution. The community is a great place to get help with troubleshooting.
- **Learning New Tips and Tricks:** Other users often share valuable tips and tricks for using the device, which can help you optimize your workflow and discover hidden features.
- **Finding Inspiration:** Seeing how other users are using their reMarkable 2 can inspire you to find new and creative ways to use the device.
- **Sharing Your Work and Getting Feedback:** You can share your notes, sketches, and other creations with the community and get feedback from other users.
- **Connecting with Other Users:** The reMarkable community is a great place to connect with other people who share your interest in the device and digital paper technology.
- **Staying Up-to-Date:** The community is often a good source of information about new software updates, features, and other reMarkable-related news.

V. Etiquette for Participating in Online Communities:

- **Be Respectful:** Treat other users with respect and courtesy.
- **Search Before Posting:** Before posting a question, search the forum or community to see if it has already been answered.
- **Provide Clear and Concise Information:** When asking for help, provide clear and concise information about the issue you are experiencing.
- **Be Patient:** Remember that people in online communities are often volunteers who are helping out in their free time.

- **Follow Community Guidelines:** Each online community has its own set of rules and guidelines. Be sure to read and follow them.

CONCLUSION

The reMarkable 2 has carved a unique niche in the digital device landscape by prioritizing a paper-like experience in a digital format. It's more than just a tablet; it's a tool designed to minimize distractions and foster deep focus, making it a powerful asset for productivity, creative expression, and document management.

The reMarkable 2 as a Tool for Focus and Productivity:

In a world saturated with notifications, alerts, and endless digital distractions, the reMarkable 2 offers a refreshing escape. Its minimalist design, monochrome E Ink display, and lack of traditional apps create an environment conducive to deep work and concentration. By removing the constant barrage of digital noise, the reMarkable 2 allows users to:

- **Focus on the Task at Hand:** Whether it's taking notes during a meeting, sketching out ideas, or reviewing a document, the reMarkable 2 helps users stay present and engaged with the task at hand.
- **Improve Productivity:** By minimizing distractions, the reMarkable 2 can help users work more efficiently and effectively. The natural writing experience also reduces the cognitive load associated with using a traditional keyboard or stylus on a glass screen.
- **Promote Deeper Thinking:** The act of writing by hand has been shown to enhance cognitive processes like memory and critical thinking. The reMarkable 2 facilitates this process in a digital format, allowing users to capture and organize their thoughts more effectively.

Embracing the Paper-Like Experience:

The core of the reMarkable 2's appeal lies in its remarkably accurate simulation of the pen-on-paper experience. This is achieved through a combination of factors:

- **E Ink Display:** The E Ink display provides a high-contrast, paper-like viewing experience that is easy on the eyes, even during extended use.
- **Textured Surface:** The textured surface of the reMarkable 2 provides a tactile feedback that closely mimics the feel of writing on paper.
- **Marker and Low Latency:** The Marker, combined with the device's low latency, creates a responsive and natural writing experience.

This paper-like experience makes the reMarkable 2 particularly well-suited for tasks that traditionally involve pen and paper, such as:

- **Note-Taking:** The reMarkable 2 offers a natural and intuitive way to take handwritten notes.
- **Sketching and Drawing:** The device's drawing tools and responsive Marker provide a satisfying creative experience.
- **Document Review and Annotation:** The reMarkable 2 makes it easy to mark up PDFs and ebooks, providing a seamless digital workflow for document review.

Future Possibilities and Updates:

reMarkable continues to improve the reMarkable 2 through software updates, adding new features, enhancing performance, and addressing user feedback. Future possibilities for the device might include:

- **Enhanced Software Features:** Improvements to handwriting recognition, search functionality, and organization tools.
- **Integration with More Services:** Expanding integration with other cloud storage services, productivity apps, or educational platforms.
- **Hardware Improvements:** Potential future hardware revisions could bring improvements to the display, battery life, or other aspects of the device.

The reMarkable 2 represents a unique approach to digital technology, focusing on creating a focused and productive environment while embracing the natural feel of pen and paper. It's a powerful tool for anyone who values focus, creativity, and a distraction-free workflow. As technology continues to evolve, the reMarkable 2 stands as a testament to the enduring appeal of the paper-like experience in a digital world.